# Vanished Skies: The Mysterious Disappearance of Amelia Earhart

Oliver Lancaster

Published by Oliver Lancaster, 2023.

While every precaution has been taken in the preparation of this book, the publisher assumes no responsibility for errors or omissions, or for damages resulting from the use of the information contained herein.

VANISHED SKIES: THE MYSTERIOUS DISAPPEARANCE OF AMELIA EARHART

**First edition. July 20, 2023.**



ISBN: 979-8223517931

Written by Oliver Lancaster.

# Also by Oliver Lancaster

Chernobyl: Unveiling the tragedy. A Comprehensive Account of the Nuclear Disaster

The Bhopal Gas Tragedy: Unraveling the Catastrophe of 1984

The Deepwater Horizon Oil Spill of 2010: A Disaster Unveiled

Fukushima Fallout: Unveiling the Truth behind the 2011 Nuclear Disaster

Minamata Disease: Poisoned Waters and the Battle for Justice (1932-1968)

Evil Women: Unmasking History's Most Notorious Women

Bundy The Dark Chronicles: America's Infamous Serial Killer

Dahmer The Dark Chronicles: America's Infamous Milwaukee Cannibal

Zodiac The Dark Chronicles: America's Infamous Cryptic Killer

Bigfoot: The Comprehensive Investigation into the Elusive Legend

Chasing Legends: The Truth behind the Chupacabra

Chasing Legends: The Truth behind the Loch Ness Monster

Aokigahara Forest: The Heartbreaking Secrets of Japan's Suicide Forest

The Amityville House: The Haunting Secrets of America's Most Infamous Residence

The Stanley Hotel: The Mystery of Colorado's Historic
Landmark
The Tower of London: The Haunted Past and Secrets of Royal
Ghosts
The Winchester Mystery House: The Riddle of Sarah
Winchester's Mansion
Vanished Skies: The Mysterious Disappearance of Amelia
Earhart


Watch for more at https://tinyurl.com/olanc.

Sign up to my free newsletter to get updates on new releases, FREE teaser chapters to upcoming releases and FREE digital short stories.

Or visit https://tinyurl.com/olanc

I never spam and you can unsubscribe at any time.

# OLIVER LANCASTER

## Disclaimer

The information presented in this book is based on extensive research and available evidence surrounding Amelia Earhart's disappearance. While efforts have been made to provide accurate and up-to-date information, readers should be aware that the mystery remains unsolved, and certain aspects of the narrative may involve speculation or differing opinions. The author and publisher cannot guarantee the absolute accuracy of all details and encourage readers to explore various sources and perspectives on the subject matter.

# Vanished Skies: The Mysterious Disappearance of Amelia Earhart

# Chapter 1: Introduction

Amelia Earhart, a name that resonates with the spirit of adventure and the pursuit of dreams, captivated the world with her daring feats in aviation during the early 20th century. Born on July 24, 1897, in Atchison, Kansas, Amelia Mary Earhart was destined to become an icon and an inspiration for generations to come. Her life was a testament to courage, determination, and a relentless desire to push the boundaries of what was deemed possible.

From a young age, Amelia exhibited a sense of curiosity and an independent spirit. She was an unconventional young woman in an era when societal expectations for women were confined to traditional roles. Amelia, however, had different aspirations. She attended Ogontz, a prestigious finishing school in Pennsylvania, where she excelled in her studies, particularly in science and athletics.

It was in 1920 when Amelia Earhart had her first taste of aviation, an experience that would forever change her life. She attended an airshow in Long Beach, California, where she took a short flight as a passenger. The exhilaration she felt during those few minutes ignited a passion within her. From that moment forward, Amelia's destiny intertwined with the skies.

In 1921, Amelia began taking flying lessons from Neta Snook, a female aviation pioneer. Despite facing financial challenges, she persevered, working as a social worker to fund her training.

On October 22, 1922, she made history by becoming the 16th woman to receive a pilot's license from the Federation Aeronautique Internationale. Amelia Earhart had embarked on a path that few women had dared to tread.

Amelia's passion for aviation was fueled by a desire to break barriers and set new records. In 1928, she was invited to become the first woman to fly across the Atlantic Ocean as a passenger in the famous Friendship flight. Although she played a supporting role in that endeavor, her ambition had been sparked. Just four years later, in 1932, Amelia Earhart made history by becoming the first woman to fly solo across the Atlantic.

Amelia's accomplishments were not limited to conquering the Atlantic Ocean. She set numerous aviation records, showcasing her skills and fearlessness. In 1935, she became the first person, regardless of gender, to fly solo from Honolulu, Hawaii, to Oakland, California. The following year, she completed a nonstop solo flight from Los Angeles to Mexico City, further solidifying her status as a pioneering aviator.

Amelia Earhart's endeavors were not only about personal achievements; she sought to empower women and challenge societal norms. She actively advocated for the involvement of women in aviation and encouraged them to pursue their dreams fearlessly. Amelia co-founded The Ninety-Nines, an organization dedicated to advancing women in aviation, which still exists today, inspiring countless women to take to the skies.

# VANISHED SKIES: THE MYSTERIOUS DISAPPEARANCE OF AMELIA EARHART

The life of Amelia Earhart was one filled with daring flights, groundbreaking records, and a relentless pursuit of adventure. Her unwavering determination and infectious enthusiasm inspired generations to chase their dreams, regardless of gender or societal expectations. As we delve deeper into the mystery surrounding her disappearance, we must first recognize and celebrate the extraordinary life of this trailblazing aviator. Amelia Earhart's legacy continues to soar through the annals of history, forever etched in the hearts of those who dare to dream and reach for the vanishing skies.

Amelia Earhart's disappearance on July 2, 1937, remains one of the most enduring and perplexing mysteries in aviation history. As the world watched in disbelief, the renowned aviator embarked on a daring flight, aiming to circumnavigate the globe along the equator. However, somewhere over the vast expanse of the Pacific Ocean, communication with Earhart's aircraft, the Lockheed Electra, ceased, and she vanished without a trace. The disappearance of Amelia Earhart gave birth to countless theories, investigations, and searches, captivating the world's attention for decades to come.

Amelia Earhart and her navigator, Fred Noonan, departed from Lae, Papua New Guinea, on July 2, 1937, heading towards Howland Island, a small, remote island in the central Pacific Ocean. Their journey was fraught with challenges, including radio communication difficulties and adverse weather conditions. As they approached Howland Island, they faced the daunting task of locating the tiny strip of land amidst the vast ocean. Tragically, all contact with Earhart's plane was lost, leaving a void of uncertainty that has puzzled investigators for over eight decades.

The mystery of Amelia Earhart's disappearance has given rise to numerous theories, each attempting to unravel the enigma. One prevailing theory suggests that Earhart's plane ran out of fuel and crashed into the ocean, leading to her demise. Despite extensive searches conducted in the aftermath, no substantial evidence was found to support this hypothesis definitively.

Another hypothesis proposes that Earhart and Noonan survived the crash and became castaways on a remote island, possibly Nikumaroro (formerly Gardner Island). This theory gained traction when artifacts were discovered on Nikumaroro in 1937, including a woman's shoe, a sextant box, and remnants of a campsite. However, subsequent searches and investigations have yielded inconclusive results, leaving this theory shrouded in uncertainty.

As with any enduring mystery, conspiracy theories have emerged, adding intrigue to the already perplexing tale of Earhart's disappearance. Some assert that Earhart was a spy for the United States, and her ill-fated flight was a cover for a covert mission. According to this theory, she was captured by the Japanese and held as a prisoner until her ultimate demise. However, extensive research and investigations have failed to provide concrete evidence to substantiate such claims.

Over the years, various tantalizing clues have surfaced, piquing the interest of investigators and amateur sleuths alike. In 1940, a British colonial officer discovered skeletal remains on

## VANISHED SKIES: THE MYSTERIOUS DISAPPEARANCE OF AMELIA EARHART

Nikumaroro, leading to speculation that they could be Amelia Earhart's. However, subsequent analysis could not conclusively confirm the identity of the remains.

In recent years, advanced technology and renewed efforts have breathed new life into the search for answers. High-resolution sonar imaging, underwater robotics, and forensic analysis have been employed to explore the depths of the Pacific Ocean in the vicinity of Earhart's projected flight path. Despite promising leads and intriguing discoveries, the ultimate fate of Amelia Earhart and Fred Noonan remains elusive.

The disappearance of Amelia Earhart continues to captivate the world's imagination, as the mystery remains unsolved. Countless expeditions, investigations, and theories have been explored, seeking to unravel the fate of this pioneering aviator. While the circumstances surrounding her disappearance may never be fully understood, Amelia Earhart's legacy as a fearless trailblazer and an inspiration to generations of dreamers and adventurers endures. The story of her disappearance serves as a reminder of the vastness and unpredictability of the world, igniting a sense of wonder and urging us to persist in our quest for answers. The enigma of Amelia Earhart's vanishing skies remains an enduring chapter in the annals of aviation history.

# OLIVER LANCASTER

# Chapter 2: Early Life and Aviation Passion

To truly understand the remarkable life of Amelia Earhart, we must delve into her formative years and the influences that shaped her indomitable spirit. Born on July 24, 1897, in Atchison, Kansas, Amelia Mary Earhart grew up in a time when societal expectations for women were vastly different from what they are today. However, her upbringing, family dynamics, and personal experiences instilled in her a sense of curiosity, independence, and a desire to break free from conventional norms.

Amelia was the daughter of Edwin Stanton Earhart and Amelia "Amy" Otis Earhart. Her childhood was marked by a supportive and nurturing family environment. Her parents encouraged her and her younger sister, Muriel, to pursue their passions and interests, irrespective of gender stereotypes prevalent at the time. This foundation of unwavering support would prove instrumental in shaping Amelia's resilience and determination.

Amelia's adventurous spirit and inquisitive nature were evident from an early age. She was often found exploring the outdoors, climbing trees, and engaging in activities typically associated with boys. Her fascination with machines and mechanics led her to dismantle and reassemble household gadgets, developing a keen understanding of how things worked. These early experiences fueled her curiosity and laid the groundwork for her later achievements in aviation.

Amelia's parents recognized her thirst for knowledge and provided her with an education that went beyond the norm for young girls at the time. She attended Hyde Park School in Chicago, Illinois, where she received a well-rounded education that nurtured her intellectual curiosity. Despite several family relocations, Amelia's parents ensured that she had access to quality education, fostering a love for learning that would shape her future endeavors.

During her childhood, Amelia had a strong support system that included influential women who served as role models. One such figure was her maternal grandmother, Amelia Harres Otis, who was a suffragette and a woman of great strength and independence. Her grandmother's progressive views undoubtedly left a lasting impact on young Amelia, instilling in her a belief in gender equality and the importance of fighting for women's rights.

It was during Amelia's teenage years that aviation began to capture the world's attention. The Wright brothers' achievements in flight fascinated her, and she followed news about aviation pioneers with great interest. However, it wasn't until she attended an airshow in California in 1920 that her passion for aviation was ignited. Taking her first flight as a passenger, the exhilaration and freedom she experienced in the skies set her on a path that would define her life.

# VANISHED SKIES: THE MYSTERIOUS DISAPPEARANCE OF AMELIA EARHART

Amelia Earhart's upbringing and early experiences challenged the prevailing gender norms of her time. She was determined to carve her own path and defy societal expectations for women. In an era when women were primarily confined to domestic roles, Amelia sought to break free from those constraints and pursue her dreams with unwavering determination.

Amelia Earhart's childhood and early influences played a crucial role in shaping the woman she would become. The supportive environment provided by her family, her innate curiosity, and the encouragement to pursue her passions set her on a trajectory that defied societal norms. Her formative years laid the foundation for the fearless aviator who would go on to inspire generations, proving that with determination and unwavering belief, one can soar to unprecedented heights. Amelia Earhart's childhood was the crucible that forged an extraordinary spirit destined to leave an indelible mark on the world of aviation.

Amelia Earhart's fascination with aviation was not a mere passing interest but a deep-rooted passion that consumed her from the moment she first set foot in an aircraft. This chapter explores the genesis of her fascination with flying, the pivotal moments that solidified her determination, and the individuals who influenced her path towards becoming one of history's most celebrated aviators.

In 1920, Amelia attended an airshow in Long Beach, California, where her life took a remarkable turn. It was here that she had her first encounter with the world of aviation.

As she soared above the earth as a passenger in an aircraft, a newfound sense of exhilaration and freedom coursed through her veins. The experience was transformative, igniting a burning desire within her to take control of the skies herself.

Fuelled by her passion, Amelia wasted no time in pursuing her dream. She sought flying lessons from Neta Snook, an accomplished female aviator, at Kinner Field in California. Despite financial constraints, she took on odd jobs to fund her training, displaying her unwavering determination to conquer the skies. Amelia proved to be a diligent and skilled student, quickly mastering the intricacies of flight.

Amelia's fascination with aviation extended beyond the thrill of flying. She became acutely aware of the gender disparities within the field. Women were largely marginalized in aviation, limited to supporting roles or relegated to the sidelines. This realization only deepened her resolve to challenge the status quo and pave the way for future generations of women aviators.

On October 22, 1922, Amelia Earhart etched her name in the annals of aviation history. With countless hours of training under her belt, she took to the skies alone, becoming the 16th woman to earn a pilot's license from the Federation Aeronautique Internationale. The exhilaration of her first solo flight solidified her commitment to aviation and propelled her towards even greater achievements.

While Amelia's initial forays into aviation were marked by personal accomplishments, she sought to push the boundaries further. In 1928, she received an invitation that would open doors to unprecedented opportunities. Joining the crew of the Friendship as a passenger, she embarked on a transatlantic crossing, becoming the first woman to undertake such a journey. This experience served as a pivotal moment, revealing the vast potential that lay before her.

Amelia Earhart's fascination with aviation reached new heights in 1932 when she embarked on a solo transatlantic flight. Just five years after her first solo flight, she shattered existing barriers and established herself as a trailblazer. Overcoming treacherous weather conditions and mechanical challenges, Amelia successfully completed the journey, becoming the first woman to fly solo across the Atlantic. This monumental achievement further fueled her passion and solidified her place in history.

Amelia Earhart's fascination with aviation was not limited to personal ambitions. She recognized the power of her achievements to inspire others, especially young women. Through her numerous public appearances, lectures, and writing, she encouraged women to break free from societal constraints, pursue their passions, and explore the skies. Amelia's unwavering dedication to promoting gender equality in aviation became an integral part of her legacy.

Amelia Earhart's fascination with aviation was a force that propelled her towards unparalleled achievements. From the transformative airshow experience to her first solo flight and groundbreaking transatlantic crossings, her unwavering determination and passion for flight set her on a trajectory of greatness. Amelia's remarkable journey not only challenged gender barriers but also inspired generations of aspiring aviators, leaving an indelible mark on the history of aviation. Her love for the skies was not only a personal calling but a beacon of hope for all those who dared to dream of soaring to new heights.

# VANISHED SKIES: THE MYSTERIOUS DISAPPEARANCE OF AMELIA EARHART

# Chapter 3: Pioneering Women in Aviation

The early days of aviation were marked by groundbreaking achievements, daring adventures, and a constant push against the boundaries of what was considered possible. In this chapter, we explore the remarkable role women played in this nascent era of flight. From pioneers like Amelia Earhart to unsung heroes, their contributions and determination shattered gender stereotypes and paved the way for generations of women to soar to new heights.

At the turn of the 20th century, aviation was an uncharted territory, a realm dominated by daring male aviators. However, women were not content to be relegated to the sidelines. Driven by a burning desire to take to the skies, they ventured into the male-dominated field, challenging societal norms and pushing the boundaries of gender roles.

One of the earliest female aviators to leave an indelible mark was Frenchwoman Raymonde de Laroche, who became the first woman in the world to receive a pilot's license in 1910. Her achievement inspired countless women to pursue aviation and demonstrated that the skies were not exclusive to men.

Amelia Earhart, as we have seen, played a pivotal role in the advancement of women in aviation. Her accomplishments and advocacy for gender equality laid the groundwork for other women to follow their dreams fearlessly. Earhart's relentless pursuit of her passion and her unwavering determination to break barriers made her a beacon of inspiration for aspiring female aviators.

In 1929, Amelia Earhart co-founded The Ninety-Nines, an organization dedicated to advancing women in aviation. Composed of licensed women pilots, this organization became a support network, a platform for sharing knowledge, and a source of encouragement for women in a field still rife with gender bias. The Ninety-Nines, which continues to thrive today, has played a vital role in nurturing talent and fostering camaraderie among women aviators.

Women in early aviation left an indelible mark through their record-breaking achievements. In 1929, Louise Thaden and Blanche Noyes became the first women to win the National Air Races, competing against their male counterparts. In 1932, aviatrix Amy Johnson set a record by becoming the first woman to fly solo from England to Australia. These and numerous other record-breaking feats shattered preconceived notions about women's abilities in aviation.

Women in early aviation faced significant challenges and resistance. They encountered skepticism, prejudice, and limited opportunities. Male aviators often dismissed their abilities and questioned their suitability for the profession. Nevertheless, these women persisted, overcoming societal barriers through sheer determination and talent.

The contributions of women in early aviation brought about a paradigm shift, leading to greater acceptance and recognition.

# VANISHED SKIES: THE MYSTERIOUS DISAPPEARANCE OF AMELIA EARHART

While gender inequalities persisted, the achievements of women in the field began to pave the way for more opportunities. Their courage and tenacity inspired a new generation of female aviators, proving that gender should never be a barrier to pursuing one's dreams.

The role of women in early aviation was one of unwavering courage, resilience, and determination. These trailblazers challenged societal norms, shattered barriers, and paved the way for future generations of women to pursue their dreams of flight. Through their accomplishments and advocacy, they demanded recognition, equality, and respect in a field traditionally dominated by men. The legacy of these early female aviators endures, reminding us of the limitless potential within each of us and the importance of breaking free from the confines of gender roles. Their contributions in aviation's formative years are a testament to the power of perseverance and the remarkable achievements that can be attained when barriers are overcome.

Amelia Earhart's name is synonymous with courage, determination, and groundbreaking achievements in the field of aviation. In this chapter, we explore the remarkable breakthroughs and milestones that marked her illustrious career. From her daring solo flights across the Atlantic to her relentless advocacy for gender equality, Amelia's accomplishments continue to inspire and shape the world of aviation.

In 1928, Amelia Earhart shattered expectations by joining the crew of the Friendship on a transatlantic flight as a passenger.

While she was not at the controls, her presence on this historic journey as the first woman to undertake a transatlantic crossing was a significant breakthrough. Amelia's participation challenged gender norms, proving that women were capable of contributing to and participating in aviation at the highest level.

Amelia Earhart's most iconic achievement came in 1932 when she boldly set out on a solo transatlantic flight. Departing from Harbor Grace, Newfoundland, on May 20, she navigated through challenging weather conditions, mechanical issues, and fatigue. Against all odds, on May 21, Amelia successfully landed in a pasture in Culmore, Northern Ireland, becoming the first woman to fly solo across the Atlantic. Her remarkable feat not only showcased her exceptional piloting skills but also shattered gender barriers, inspiring women worldwide to pursue their dreams fearlessly.

Amelia Earhart's passion for pushing the boundaries of aviation extended far beyond her solo transatlantic flight. She embarked on numerous record-breaking flights, further cementing her place in aviation history. In 1935, she became the first person, regardless of gender, to fly solo from Honolulu, Hawaii, to Oakland, California. The following year, she set another record by completing a nonstop solo flight from Los Angeles to Mexico City. Amelia's remarkable achievements demonstrated her skill, determination, and commitment to constantly surpassing expectations.

Amelia Earhart's most ambitious and fateful undertaking was her ill-fated attempt to circumnavigate the globe. On June 1,

1937, she set off from Oakland, California, in her Lockheed Electra aircraft, aiming to complete the journey along the equator. While the flight ended tragically with her disappearance, it is a testament to Amelia's unwavering spirit and her willingness to embrace challenges that were previously thought insurmountable.

Amelia Earhart's achievements extended beyond her groundbreaking flights. She tirelessly advocated for gender equality in aviation, using her platform to inspire and uplift women. Through her public appearances, lectures, and writings, she encouraged women to break free from societal constraints and pursue careers in aviation. Amelia's unwavering belief in the capabilities of women and her dedication to empowering them laid the foundation for future generations of female aviators.

Amelia Earhart's breakthroughs and achievements left an indelible mark on the world of aviation. Her daring solo flights, record-breaking accomplishments, and tireless advocacy inspired countless individuals, both men and women, to pursue their dreams and defy limitations. Amelia's legacy continues to resonate, reminding us that no dream is too lofty and no obstacle insurmountable. Her unwavering spirit and determination to push boundaries and challenge gender norms serve as a constant source of inspiration for those who dare to reach for the skies.

Amelia Earhart's breakthroughs and achievements in aviation epitomize the spirit of adventure, courage, and resilience. From her solo transatlantic flight to her unwavering advocacy for women in aviation, she blazed a trail that defied expectations and set new standards. Amelia's relentless pursuit of her dreams and her unwavering belief in the potential of women continues to inspire generations, propelling the field of aviation forward and reminding us that boundaries exist only to be surpassed. Her breakthroughs and achievements remain a testament to the power of determination, passion, and the enduring legacy of one of history's most celebrated aviators.

# VANISHED SKIES: THE MYSTERIOUS DISAPPEARANCE OF AMELIA EARHART

# Chapter 4: Transatlantic Flight and Stardom

Amelia Earhart's solo transatlantic flight stands as one of the most remarkable achievements in aviation history. In this chapter, we delve into the details of this historic journey, from the preparation and challenges she faced to the ultimate triumph that forever solidified her place as a pioneering aviator.

Amelia Earhart's decision to undertake a solo transatlantic flight was driven by her insatiable thirst for adventure and her unwavering determination to conquer new frontiers. On May 20, 1932, she embarked on her quest, departing from Harbor Grace, Newfoundland, aboard her Lockheed Vega aircraft, named the "Friendship."

The solo transatlantic flight presented numerous challenges that Amelia had to navigate with skill and courage. As she ventured into the vast expanse of the Atlantic Ocean, she encountered severe weather conditions, including strong winds, fog, and icy temperatures. These elements tested her resolve and required meticulous planning and precise navigation.

Amelia Earhart's solo transatlantic flight was a pioneering endeavor in many respects. She employed innovative navigation techniques, relying on celestial observations, dead reckoning, and radio communications to guide her course. At a time when modern navigation tools were limited, her ability to navigate with precision showcased her exceptional skill and resourcefulness.

During her solo transatlantic flight, Amelia faced grueling physical and mental challenges. With no co-pilot or crew for support, she endured long hours in the cockpit, battling fatigue, loneliness, and the constant hum of her aircraft's engine. However, her unwavering determination and relentless spirit pushed her forward, propelling her closer to her destination.

Amelia Earhart's solo transatlantic flight reached its climax on May 21, 1932, when she touched down in a pasture near Derrygimla, in County Galway, Ireland. The world celebrated her arrival, recognizing her as the first woman to successfully complete a solo transatlantic flight. The significance of her achievement reverberated across continents, inspiring generations of aviators and defying prevailing gender norms.

Amelia Earhart's record-breaking flight served as a symbol of women's empowerment and the ability to transcend societal expectations. Her accomplishment shattered the belief that aviation was an exclusively male domain, inspiring women worldwide to pursue their dreams fearlessly. Amelia became an icon, embodying courage, determination, and the unyielding spirit of breaking barriers.

Amelia Earhart's solo transatlantic flight left an indelible mark on the history of aviation. Her achievement paved the way for future generations of women aviators, proving that gender should never limit one's aspirations. It ignited a flame of possibility and empowerment, encouraging women to strive for greatness in any field they chose.

Amelia Earhart's solo transatlantic flight not only made her a trailblazer in aviation but also transformed her into an international inspiration. Her courage and accomplishments inspired individuals of all backgrounds to dream big and defy limitations. Her journey symbolized the human capacity to conquer challenges, reminding us that the sky is not the limit when it comes to our aspirations.

Amelia Earhart's record-breaking solo transatlantic flight was a testament to her unwavering determination, pioneering spirit, and exceptional skill as an aviator. Her successful journey across the vast Atlantic Ocean shattered gender barriers and inspired countless individuals to reach for their own personal triumphs. Amelia's accomplishment stands as an enduring symbol of human resilience and the power of pushing beyond perceived limitations. Her solo transatlantic flight forever etched her name in the annals of aviation history and solidified her status as a true trailblazer.

Amelia Earhart's record-breaking achievements in aviation catapulted her to worldwide fame. In this chapter, we explore the intense media attention and the profound impact she had on popular culture. From her captivating personality to her trailblazing feats, Amelia became an icon, captivating the imagination of people around the globe.

Amelia Earhart's accomplishments captured the attention of the media like few others of her time. Her solo transatlantic flight in 1932 thrust her into the international spotlight, earning her a place among the world's most celebrated aviators. Newspapers, magazines, and radio stations clamored to cover her extraordinary achievements, making her a household name.

Amelia's story resonated deeply with people from all walks of life. Her courage, determination, and willingness to defy societal expectations made her an inspiration to millions. The media played a crucial role in disseminating her message and spreading her story, igniting the imaginations of individuals who dared to dream of adventure and achievement.

Amelia Earhart's ascent to fame had a profound impact on women across the globe. She became a symbol of empowerment and the epitome of breaking gender barriers. Her success demonstrated that women were capable of achieving greatness in male-dominated fields. Women from all corners of society looked up to her as a role model, a beacon of possibility, and a reminder that their dreams were valid and attainable.

Amelia's fame attracted the attention of prominent figures in various industries. She collaborated with fashion designers, endorsing products and appearing in advertisements, which helped solidify her image as a trendsetter and a style icon. Her endorsement of functional clothing and accessories for women in aviation further emphasized her influence beyond the skies.

Amelia Earhart's celebrity status extended beyond aviation. She penned several books about her experiences, sharing her perspectives and adventures with a captivated audience. Her literary endeavors further propelled her fame and positioned her as an authoritative voice in aviation and women's empowerment. Amelia also embarked on speaking tours, captivating audiences with her eloquence, wit, and inspirational messages.

Amelia's fame and media attention extended far beyond the aviation community. She represented the spirit of adventure and the pursuit of dreams, resonating with people from all walks of life. Her image adorned posters, magazines, and newspapers, becoming an enduring cultural icon of the era. Amelia's influence seeped into music, film, and literature, leaving an indelible mark on popular culture.

Amelia Earhart's disappearance in 1937 only heightened her fame and solidified her status as an enigmatic figure. The mystery surrounding her vanishing skies further perpetuated her legend, captivating the media and the public. Countless theories, investigations, and searches emerged, each adding another layer to her enduring legacy.

Even decades after her disappearance, Amelia Earhart's fame and the media attention surrounding her accomplishments continue to resonate. She remains an icon of perseverance, courage, and breaking barriers. Her life and story serve as a reminder to embrace adventure, challenge the status quo, and fearlessly pursue our passions, regardless of the obstacles we may face.

Amelia Earhart's fame and the media attention she received were a testament to her extraordinary achievements and the profound impact she had on society. Her rise to fame inspired generations of individuals, especially women, to believe in their capabilities and strive for greatness. Through her media presence, she became an emblem of courage, determination, and the enduring spirit of human achievement. Amelia Earhart's legacy continues to shine brightly, reminding us of the transformative power of perseverance, and the ability to capture the imagination of a global audience.

# VANISHED SKIES: THE MYSTERIOUS DISAPPEARANCE OF AMELIA EARHART

# Chapter 5: Ambitious Dreams and Circumnavigation Plans

Amelia Earhart's insatiable thirst for adventure and her relentless pursuit of aviation excellence led her to embark on a monumental quest: to become the first person to circumnavigate the globe along the equator. In this chapter, we explore Amelia's aspirations, the challenges she faced, and the indomitable spirit that propelled her towards this daring endeavor.

Amelia Earhart's ambition to circumnavigate the globe began to take shape long before she announced her plans publicly. Inspired by the achievements of other aviators and driven by her own desire to push the boundaries of what was deemed possible, she conceived the audacious goal of flying around the world, charting new territory in the field of aviation.

Amelia meticulously planned her ambitious journey, considering various factors such as aircraft, fueling logistics, navigation, and weather conditions. She selected the Lockheed Electra, a twin-engine aircraft known for its reliability and range. With the support of her team, she prepared extensively, conducting test flights and fine-tuning her equipment for the long and challenging voyage ahead.

Amelia's planned circumnavigation route aimed to encircle the globe along the equator, covering approximately 29,000 miles. Departing from Oakland, California, she would fly eastward, making stops in various countries and continents, ultimately returning to California to complete the historic journey. This route would take her through diverse landscapes, challenging weather patterns, and unfamiliar territories.

Amelia's quest for circumnavigation was not without its challenges and risks. The journey would test her endurance, navigational skills, and resilience. She would encounter unpredictable weather, vast stretches of open ocean, unfamiliar airstrips, and communication difficulties. Moreover, the limitations of aviation technology at the time added an element of uncertainty to the expedition.

Amelia's aspirations to circumnavigate the globe went beyond personal accomplishment. She understood the power of her journey to inspire and empower future generations of aviators, especially women. By challenging the status quo and pushing the boundaries of what was perceived as possible, Amelia aimed to inspire individuals worldwide to pursue their dreams, regardless of gender or societal expectations.

Tragically, Amelia Earhart's quest to circumnavigate the globe ended in mystery and uncertainty. On July 2, 1937, during the leg of her journey from Lae, Papua New Guinea, to Howland Island, her Lockheed Electra disappeared over the vast expanse of the Pacific Ocean. The circumstances surrounding her disappearance sparked numerous theories, investigations, and searches that continue to captivate the world's attention to this day.

# VANISHED SKIES: THE MYSTERIOUS DISAPPEARANCE OF AMELIA EARHART

While Amelia's aspiration to circumnavigate the globe remained unfulfilled, her indomitable spirit and determination continue to inspire. Her quest symbolized the human drive for exploration, adventure, and the pursuit of dreams. Her unwavering belief in the power of aviation and her relentless pursuit of pushing boundaries left an indelible legacy, inspiring countless individuals to chart their own paths, embrace challenges, and strive for greatness.

Though Amelia's personal quest to circumnavigate the globe may have been cut short, her spirit lives on in the countless aviators who have followed in her footsteps. The desire to conquer the globe continues to drive pilots to take on circumnavigation flights, paying homage to Amelia's groundbreaking aspirations. Her unfulfilled quest remains a testament to the resilience of the human spirit and the enduring pursuit of adventure.

Amelia Earhart's aspirations to circumnavigate the globe exemplified her unwavering determination, courage, and relentless pursuit of aviation excellence. Her quest to conquer the world's skies along the equator represented the epitome of adventure and the pursuit of dreams. While the outcome of her endeavor may forever be shrouded in mystery, her legacy as a trailblazing aviator and an inspiration to generations of adventurers continues to soar. Amelia's aspirations remain an enduring testament to the power of ambition and the transformative potential of pushing beyond perceived limits.

Amelia Earhart's quest to circumnavigate the globe along the equator was marked by a myriad of challenges and meticulous preparations. In this chapter, we delve into the obstacles she faced and the extensive measures taken to ensure a safe and successful journey.

Amelia's ambitious endeavor to fly around the world posed numerous challenges. One of the primary obstacles was navigating through unfamiliar territories and vast stretches of open ocean. The lack of advanced navigational aids at the time meant relying on celestial observations, dead reckoning, and rudimentary radio communication for course plotting and determining positions.

The global circumnavigation presented Amelia with a range of weather and climate conditions that she had to navigate. She would encounter treacherous storms, unpredictable wind patterns, extreme temperatures, and varying weather systems. Her route would take her through diverse regions, from tropical heat to Arctic cold, demanding adaptability and skill to mitigate the effects of adverse weather.

A critical challenge in Amelia's journey was fueling and resupplying her aircraft, the Lockheed Electra, at various locations along the route. This required meticulous planning and coordination to ensure the availability of fuel and necessary provisions in remote and unfamiliar regions. Limited infrastructure and resources in some areas posed additional logistical challenges.

Preparing the Lockheed Electra for the arduous journey involved modifications and enhancements to optimize its performance and endurance. The aircraft's fuel capacity was expanded to increase its range, and additional navigation and communication equipment were installed. The team worked meticulously to ensure the aircraft was in optimal condition, addressing potential mechanical issues and conducting rigorous testing.

Planning the circumnavigation route was a complex task, involving considerations of political boundaries, airspace restrictions, and diplomatic negotiations. Amelia and her team collaborated with experts and authorities to chart a course that would maximize safety and minimize bureaucratic hurdles. Securing permissions to land and refuel at various international airports required diplomatic efforts and meticulous coordination.

Embarking on a grueling journey like circumnavigation demanded physical and mental preparedness. Amelia underwent rigorous training, including physical fitness regimens and endurance exercises. She honed her piloting skills, practiced emergency procedures, and familiarized herself with the aircraft's systems. Mental resilience and psychological readiness were essential to withstand the demands of long flights, isolation, and the potential challenges that lay ahead.

Preparing for unforeseen circumstances and emergencies was paramount. Amelia and her team developed contingency plans and emergency protocols to address potential scenarios such as mechanical failures, adverse weather conditions, and medical emergencies. They equipped the aircraft with survival gear, communication devices, and emergency provisions, ensuring Amelia's safety and well-being throughout the journey.

Amelia's quest would not have been possible without the support of a dedicated team. She relied on skilled mechanics, navigators, meteorologists, and ground support personnel who provided crucial assistance in planning, logistics, and maintaining the aircraft. Access to accurate weather information, navigational charts, and communication systems was vital for her safety and successful navigation.

Amelia Earhart's journey to circumnavigate the globe was a formidable undertaking that required meticulous preparations and the ability to overcome diverse challenges. From navigating unknown territories and adverse weather conditions to ensuring fueling and resupply along the route, every aspect of the journey demanded careful planning and execution. Amelia's meticulous preparations, coupled with her indomitable spirit, paved the way for her groundbreaking attempt to conquer the world's skies. Her commitment to safety, her dedicated team, and her unwavering determination were instrumental in laying the groundwork for the historic adventure that would captivate the world's attention.

# VANISHED SKIES: THE MYSTERIOUS DISAPPEARANCE OF AMELIA EARHART

# Chapter 6: Earhart's Final Flight: The Itinerary

Amelia Earhart's ambitious goal of circumnavigating the globe along the equator required careful planning of the flight path and strategic stopovers. In this chapter, we explore the intended route Amelia aimed to follow and the significant locations where she planned to make crucial pit stops during her historic journey.

Amelia's intended flight path aimed to cover approximately 29,000 miles, circumnavigating the globe along the equator. Departing from Oakland, California, she would fly eastward, making stops in various countries and continents before returning to California to complete the historic journey. The route would take her through diverse landscapes, spanning oceans, continents, and remote regions.

After departing from California, Amelia's first significant stopover was planned in Miami, Florida. This served as a logistical and strategic hub, allowing her to finalize preparations, conduct any necessary adjustments to the aircraft, and ensure that all systems were functioning optimally before embarking on the long journey over the Atlantic Ocean.

From Miami, Amelia intended to fly south, making several stops along the eastern coast of South America. Locations such as Natal, Brazil, and Paramaribo, Suriname, were among the planned stopovers. These stops would provide opportunities for refueling, rest, and potential interactions with local aviation communities.

Continuing eastward, Amelia planned to touch down in Africa, specifically in the British colony of Gambia. The stopover in Bathurst (now Banjul) was vital for refueling and gathering provisions before venturing across the vast expanse of the African continent.

From Africa, Amelia intended to fly across the Indian Ocean and make a series of stops in India and Southeast Asia. Rangoon (now Yangon), Myanmar, and Bangkok, Thailand, were among the planned stopovers. These locations would provide crucial refueling and rest opportunities as she continued her eastward journey.

One of the most significant stretches of the journey would take Amelia across Australia and the vast expanse of the Pacific Ocean. Darwin, Australia, was a planned stopover before the challenging leg across the Pacific. A crucial stopover was also planned on Howland Island, a small remote coral island in the Pacific, for refueling and preparing for the challenging flight to Hawaii.

After successfully crossing the Pacific, Amelia aimed to make a stopover in Honolulu, Hawaii. This would serve as a momentous milestone, marking the completion of the most challenging and treacherous part of her journey. From Hawaii, Amelia would continue her westward flight, making stops in California and completing her circumnavigation at Oakland, the starting point of her historic adventure.

# VANISHED SKIES: THE MYSTERIOUS DISAPPEARANCE OF AMELIA EARHART

Amelia Earhart's intended flight path and strategic stopovers showcased the sheer scale and diversity of her journey. From the United States to South America, Africa, India, Southeast Asia, Australia, and the Pacific, her route spanned continents and oceans. The planned stopovers provided essential refueling, rest, and logistical support, allowing Amelia to continue her quest to conquer the globe. Each location held significance, adding layers of adventure and challenge to her historic expedition. While her journey ended prematurely, the intended flight path and stopovers remain a testament to Amelia's ambition, resilience, and determination to leave an indelible mark on the world of aviation.

Amelia Earhart's quest to circumnavigate the globe necessitated significant modifications to her aircraft, the Lockheed Electra. In this chapter, we explore the engineering advancements and adjustments made to enhance the aircraft's performance, endurance, and safety for the historic journey.

One crucial modification made to the Lockheed Electra was the expansion of its fuel capacity. To increase the aircraft's range and reduce the number of refueling stops, additional fuel tanks were installed. This modification allowed Amelia to cover longer distances and navigate remote regions where fueling options might be limited or unavailable.

Equipping the aircraft with advanced navigation and communication equipment was essential for the success and safety of the circumnavigation. The Lockheed Electra was outfitted with cutting-edge technology for the time, including radio direction finders, radio transmitters, and receivers. These instruments allowed Amelia to communicate with ground stations, receive weather updates, and navigate through various terrains.

To alleviate pilot fatigue during the long flights, an autopilot system was installed in the Lockheed Electra. The system provided limited automation, allowing the aircraft to maintain a steady course while Amelia could focus on other critical tasks such as navigation, communication, and monitoring the aircraft's performance.

Given the remote regions and vast expanses of ocean that Amelia would cross, long-range radio equipment was crucial for communication and distress signaling. The Lockheed Electra was equipped with powerful radio transmitters and receivers capable of transmitting signals over great distances. This enabled Amelia to maintain communication with ground stations and other aircraft, ensuring her safety and providing a lifeline in case of emergencies.

In preparation for the possibility of unexpected situations or forced landings, the aircraft was equipped with survival and emergency equipment. This included items such as life rafts, emergency rations, first aid supplies, and signaling devices. These provisions were vital for Amelia's safety and well-being in the event of an emergency or a forced landing in remote or inhospitable environments.

Given the unpredictability of weather conditions along the intended route, the Lockheed Electra was equipped with additional weather instruments. These instruments included barometers, anemometers, and thermometers to measure atmospheric pressure, wind speed, and temperature. Accurate weather information allowed Amelia to make informed decisions regarding flight paths and potential weather-related challenges.

To withstand the rigors of long-distance flying and potential rough landings, the landing gear of the Lockheed Electra was reinforced and strengthened. This modification aimed to enhance the durability of the aircraft's undercarriage, ensuring its ability to handle various landing surfaces, including rough airstrips in remote locations.

To maximize fuel efficiency and enhance the aircraft's performance, weight reduction measures were implemented. Non-essential equipment and furnishings were removed or minimized to reduce the overall weight of the aircraft. This optimization allowed for increased fuel capacity and improved flight characteristics, ensuring the Lockheed Electra could handle the demands of the circumnavigation.

The modifications made to Amelia Earhart's aircraft, the Lockheed Electra, were instrumental in preparing it for the extraordinary demands of her circumnavigation attempt. Enhanced fuel capacity, advanced navigation and communication equipment, survival provisions, and weight reduction measures were among the key adjustments made. These engineering advancements aimed to optimize the aircraft's performance, increase its endurance, and ensure Amelia's safety throughout her historic journey. The modifications made to the Lockheed Electra reflected the innovative spirit of the time and the dedication to pushing the boundaries of aviation technology. They were a testament to the collaborative efforts of engineers, aviators, and technicians who worked tirelessly to prepare Amelia and her aircraft for the daring adventure that would captivate the world's attention.

# VANISHED SKIES: THE MYSTERIOUS DISAPPEARANCE OF AMELIA EARHART

# Chapter 7: Departure from Miami

Amelia Earhart's departure for her historic circumnavigation journey was the culmination of meticulous planning, preparations, and the convergence of numerous significant events. In this chapter, we explore the key milestones and events that led up to Amelia's departure, marking the beginning of her epic adventure.

The announcement of Amelia Earhart's intention to circumnavigate the globe along the equator created a wave of excitement and anticipation. News of her ambitious quest spread rapidly, capturing the imagination of people worldwide. The public eagerly awaited updates on her preparations, routing, and the daring endeavor she was about to undertake.

In the months leading up to her departure, Amelia conducted preparatory flights and engaged in extensive training to ensure she was fully prepared for the challenges that lay ahead. She flew practice missions, honing her skills in navigation, endurance, and emergency procedures. These flights also allowed her to fine-tune the aircraft's performance and assess its suitability for the demanding journey.

Amelia Earhart collaborated closely with a team of experts, including navigators, engineers, meteorologists, and aviation authorities, to ensure the success and safety of her circumnavigation. These collaborations involved consultations, briefings, and assessments of the intended route, weather patterns, and logistical considerations. Additionally, sponsors provided support in terms of funding, equipment, and resources to facilitate her historic flight.

The media played a significant role in documenting Amelia's preparations and generating publicity for her journey. Newspapers, magazines, and radio stations provided regular updates on her progress, amplifying her story and generating widespread interest. Interviews, press conferences, and public appearances further fueled public fascination with Amelia's impending departure, making her a household name.

In the weeks leading up to her departure, the Lockheed Electra underwent final equipment checks and modifications. Every aspect of the aircraft was meticulously inspected to ensure it was in optimal condition. Mechanical systems were tested, instruments calibrated, and safety measures reviewed to mitigate any potential issues during the journey.

As part of her preparations, Amelia embarked on a goodwill tour, visiting various cities and engaging with aviation communities and supporters. These visits provided an opportunity to inspire and garner encouragement from fellow aviators and the general public. The overwhelming support Amelia received further fueled her determination and boosted morale as she prepared to embark on her historic adventure.

A farewell ceremony was held to mark Amelia Earhart's imminent departure. The event brought together friends, family, sponsors, aviation enthusiasts, and well-wishers to bid her farewell and offer words of encouragement. The ceremony symbolized the culmination of months of hard work, planning, and anticipation, signaling the beginning of a remarkable journey.

The day of Amelia Earhart's departure was met with great fanfare and media coverage. Crowds gathered to witness the historic moment as she climbed aboard the Lockheed Electra, ready to embark on her daring circumnavigation. Amid cheers and applause, the engines roared to life, and the aircraft taxied down the runway, signaling the start of Amelia's epic adventure.

The events leading up to Amelia Earhart's departure for her historic circumnavigation were marked by excitement, preparation, and the collective support of numerous individuals and organizations. The public's anticipation, media coverage, preparatory flights, collaborations with experts, and final equipment checks all contributed to the momentous occasion. As Amelia took to the skies, she carried with her the hopes and dreams of countless individuals inspired by her courage, determination, and unwavering spirit. The events leading up to her departure set the stage for the extraordinary journey that would capture the world's attention and forever etch her name in the annals of aviation history.

The initial stages of Amelia Earhart's ill-fated flight marked the beginning of her ambitious quest to circumnavigate the globe along the equator. In this chapter, we delve into the early moments of her journey, from the departure in Oakland to the challenging segments across the Pacific, leading up to the unfortunate events that would forever cast a shadow of mystery over her historic flight.

On June 1, 1937, amidst great anticipation and media coverage, Amelia Earhart's journey began as she departed from Oakland, California. The Lockheed Electra taxied down the runway, its engines roaring, as a crowd of well-wishers and aviation enthusiasts bid her farewell. The atmosphere was charged with excitement, and the world watched as she embarked on her daring adventure.

After departing from Oakland, Amelia made a stopover in Tucson, Arizona, to refuel and prepare for the long journey ahead. From there, she continued to Miami, Florida, where the Lockheed Electra underwent final checks and adjustments. These early stopovers allowed for necessary maintenance and ensured the aircraft's readiness for the challenging flights that awaited her.

Amelia's first major hurdle was crossing the Atlantic Ocean. Departing from Miami on June 1, she successfully flew to San Juan, Puerto Rico, where she made her first stopover in the Caribbean. Continuing eastward, she made stops in Venezuela and Brazil, overcoming challenges posed by diverse weather patterns, unfamiliar landing strips, and logistical considerations in remote regions.

The next leg of Amelia's journey took her across the South Atlantic from Natal, Brazil, to Dakar, Senegal, in Africa. This was a critical and challenging segment, spanning over 2,500 miles of open ocean. The flight tested her navigation skills, endurance, and the limits of her aircraft's capabilities. Successfully reaching Dakar marked a significant milestone and brought her closer to completing the African leg of the journey.

From Senegal, Amelia flew across the African continent, making stops in Libreville (Gabon), Brazzaville (Congo), and Khartoum (Sudan). These stopovers provided essential refueling and maintenance opportunities in regions with limited infrastructure. Continuing eastward, she crossed the Indian Ocean, navigating through challenging weather conditions, and reached the British colony of Gambia, where she prepared for the subsequent leg of her journey.

Amelia's circumnavigation continued as she flew across India, making stops in Calcutta (now Kolkata), Rangoon (now Yangon), Bangkok, and Singapore. These vibrant cities provided essential rest and refueling opportunities before venturing into the challenging Pacific leg of the journey. Amelia's progress captivated the public's attention, and her courage and determination continued to inspire people around the world.

After departing from Singapore, Amelia set her sights on Australia, planning to make a stopover in Darwin. The subsequent leg of the journey across the vast Pacific Ocean was one of the most daunting challenges she faced. The flight to Howland Island, a remote coral atoll, would test her endurance, navigation skills, and the capabilities of her aircraft to the utmost.

On July 2, 1937, Amelia Earhart and her navigator, Fred Noonan, took off from Lae, Papua New Guinea, en route to

Howland Island. Unfortunately, they never reached their destination. Despite extensive search and rescue efforts, no trace of the aircraft or its occupants was found. The ill-fated disappearance of Amelia Earhart remains one of aviation's greatest mysteries, leaving unanswered questions and fueling speculation and theories for decades to come.

The initial stages of Amelia Earhart's ill-fated flight were marked by determination, challenges, and progress towards her goal of circumnavigating the globe. From the departure in Oakland to the crossings of the Atlantic, Africa, India, and Southeast Asia, Amelia displayed her remarkable piloting skills and unwavering spirit. However, the tragic turn of events that led to her disappearance over the Pacific Ocean would forever cast a shadow of mystery and uncertainty over her historic journey. Despite the unanswered questions, Amelia's courage, ambition, and pioneering spirit continue to inspire generations of aviators and dreamers who dare to push the boundaries of what is possible in the world of aviation.

# VANISHED SKIES: THE MYSTERIOUS DISAPPEARANCE OF AMELIA EARHART

# Chapter 8: Lost over the Pacific: The Vanishing Act

The last known communications with Amelia Earhart form a crucial piece of the puzzle surrounding her ill-fated flight. In this chapter, we delve into the final messages exchanged between Amelia and ground stations, shedding light on the events leading up to her disappearance and the enduring mystery that surrounds her final moments.

On July 2, 1937, Amelia Earhart and her navigator, Fred Noonan, departed from Lae, Papua New Guinea, in their attempt to reach Howland Island. As they took off, radio transmissions confirmed their departure and set the stage for the critical communications that would follow.

Throughout the journey, radio communication was essential for Amelia's navigation and relaying vital information to ground stations. However, radio transmissions during the Pacific crossing proved to be challenging. Amelia and Fred Noonan experienced difficulties in establishing consistent contact due to a combination of factors, including the vast expanse of the ocean, limited radio equipment capabilities, and atmospheric interference.

The US Coast Guard cutter, the USS Itasca, stationed near Howland Island, played a crucial role in providing communication support for Amelia's flight. Equipped with advanced radio equipment, the Itasca established a radio frequency and acted as a navigational guide for Amelia, relaying critical information and instructions for her approach to Howland Island.

In the early stages of the Pacific crossing, Amelia's communications with the Itasca were relatively regular. She reported her position and received updates on weather conditions and guidance for her approach to Howland Island. The Itasca provided crucial support in navigating towards the intended destination, maintaining contact as they drew closer.

As Amelia Earhart and Fred Noonan neared Howland Island, their communications with the Itasca became increasingly sporadic. Fading radio signals and static interference hindered effective communication, making it difficult for both parties to establish a clear and consistent connection. These challenges added complexity and uncertainty to the navigation process.

The last known communications from Amelia were desperate and indicated the increasing urgency of the situation. In her final messages, she expressed frustration with receiving bearings from the Itasca, citing difficulty in hearing the signals clearly. Time became a critical factor, and Amelia's messages reflected a sense of urgency as she sought to establish a clear line of communication and pinpoint her exact location.

Following the final messages, Amelia Earhart and Fred Noonan vanished over the vast Pacific Ocean. Despite extensive search efforts, no trace of their aircraft or the occupants was found. Unanswered distress calls and silence perpetuated the mystery surrounding their fate, leaving the world with unanswered questions about the events that unfolded during their ill-fated flight.

The last known communications with Amelia Earhart continue to captivate the imagination and fuel speculation about the circumstances surrounding her disappearance. Various theories and hypotheses have emerged, ranging from running out of fuel to navigational errors or forced landings on uninhabited islands. However, the truth of what transpired during those final moments remains elusive, shrouding Amelia Earhart's fate in enduring mystery.

The last known communications with Amelia Earhart provide glimpses into the challenges she faced during her ill-fated flight. Fading signals, radio interference, and the increasing urgency of her messages paint a picture of a desperate situation. The unanswered distress calls and the subsequent disappearance over the vast expanse of the Pacific Ocean have given rise to numerous theories and speculation. The final communications with Amelia Earhart serve as a haunting reminder of the enduring mystery that surrounds her disappearance, leaving the world to wonder about the fate of one of aviation's most iconic figures.

Amelia Earhart's disappearance over the Pacific Ocean on July 2, 1937, has sparked numerous theories and speculation about the events that unfolded during her ill-fated flight. In this chapter, we explore some of the most prominent theories surrounding her disappearance, each offering a unique perspective on the enduring mystery that surrounds Amelia Earhart.

**Theory 1: Crash and Sinking at Sea:**

One prevailing theory suggests that Amelia Earhart's plane crashed into the Pacific Ocean, and she and Fred Noonan perished at sea. According to this theory, the aircraft may have experienced a navigational error, fuel exhaustion, or encountered adverse weather conditions, leading to a forced landing on the water. The plane is believed to have sunk, leaving no physical trace.

**Theory 2: Capture and Death in Japanese Territory:**

Another theory proposes that Amelia Earhart and Fred Noonan were captured by the Japanese government after landing in the Marshall Islands, which were under Japanese control at the time. According to this theory, they were taken into custody, potentially as spies, and subsequently died in captivity. Some claim that the US government was aware of their fate but chose to cover it up.

**Theory 3: Crash Landing on Nikumaroro Island:**

One theory suggests that Amelia Earhart and Fred Noonan made a crash landing on Nikumaroro Island, now part of the Republic of Kiribati. It is believed that they survived the initial landing but eventually perished on the uninhabited island due to a lack of resources and exposure to the elements. Searches and investigations have been conducted on Nikumaroro Island in an attempt to find evidence supporting this theory.

**Theory 4: Secret Spy Mission:**

Speculation has also arisen that Amelia Earhart's circumnavigation attempt was a cover for a secret spy mission on behalf of the US government. According to this theory, her disappearance was a result of her involvement in espionage activities. Proponents of this theory argue that her flight route and communication difficulties were intentional, aimed at covert operations rather than a genuine circumnavigation.

## Theory 5: Living Under a New Identity:

A less conventional theory suggests that Amelia Earhart survived the flight and chose to live under a new identity. Supporters of this theory propose that she may have intentionally disappeared to escape public scrutiny, forging a new life elsewhere. However, the lack of concrete evidence and the challenges of maintaining such a secret identity for an extended period make this theory highly speculative.

## Theory 6: Technical Failure and Forced Landing:

This theory proposes that technical failures, such as engine malfunctions or navigational instrument issues, led to a forced landing on an unknown or uncharted island. According to this theory, Amelia and Fred survived the landing but were unable to attract attention or rescue due to their remote location. The absence of radio communications and the aircraft's disappearance would be attributed to the plane's eventual destruction.

Theories surrounding Amelia Earhart's disappearance continue to captivate the public's imagination, as each theory offers its own narrative to explain the enigma. Whether it's the crash and sinking at sea, capture by the Japanese, a crash landing on an uninhabited island, involvement in espionage, living under a new identity, or technical failure and forced landing, each theory reflects the complexity of the mystery and the lack of concrete evidence.

Despite extensive search efforts, no definitive answers have emerged, leaving Amelia Earhart's fate and the circumstances surrounding her disappearance as one of aviation's greatest unsolved mysteries. The allure of uncovering the truth and resolving the unanswered questions surrounding her ill-fated flight continues to inspire speculation, investigation, and ongoing searches. As the world awaits further discoveries or breakthroughs, the theories surrounding Amelia Earhart's disappearance keep her legacy alive and ensure that her story remains an enduring enigma in the history of aviation.

# VANISHED SKIES: THE MYSTERIOUS DISAPPEARANCE OF AMELIA EARHART

# Chapter 9: The Search and Rescue Efforts

The disappearance of Amelia Earhart in 1937 sparked an extensive and ongoing search effort to uncover the truth behind her fate. In this chapter, we explore the various search missions conducted in the aftermath of her disappearance, highlighting the dedicated efforts to solve the enduring mystery surrounding Amelia Earhart.

Immediately following Amelia Earhart's disappearance, a massive search and rescue operation was launched by the United States Coast Guard, Navy, and civilian organizations. The search initially focused on the vicinity of Howland Island, the intended destination of her ill-fated flight. Ships, aircraft, and personnel scoured the vast Pacific Ocean in an attempt to locate any signs of Amelia, Fred Noonan, or their aircraft.

In the weeks and months that followed, the search expanded to encompass a wider area, including coastal regions and remote islands. Multiple search missions were conducted, utilizing both aerial reconnaissance and surface vessels. Areas of interest included the Phoenix Islands, the Gilbert Islands, the Marshall Islands, and various other islands and atolls in the Pacific. Unfortunately, these searches yielded no conclusive evidence of Amelia's whereabouts.

In more recent years, several private expeditions have been undertaken under the banner of the Earhart Project, seeking to uncover new leads and evidence. These expeditions have focused on specific locations such as Nikumaroro Island (formerly Gardner Island) in the Republic of Kiribati. Through advanced technology, underwater searches, and archaeological investigations, these expeditions have aimed to find artifacts or remnants that could shed light on Amelia's disappearance.

Sonar surveys and underwater exploration have been utilized in search efforts to detect potential wreckage of the Lockheed Electra. These methods involve utilizing advanced sonar technology to map the ocean floor and identify any anomalies that may indicate the presence of the lost aircraft. While some promising leads have been identified, extensive searches of the oceanic regions have yet to produce conclusive results.

In conjunction with search missions, forensic analysis and anthropological research have played a role in attempting to identify human remains or artifacts that could be connected to Amelia Earhart and Fred Noonan. These efforts have involved examining bones, DNA analysis, and comparing historical records to physical evidence, with the aim of establishing a definitive link to their disappearance.

The search missions for Amelia Earhart have fostered collaborations and international cooperation among organizations, governments, and experts worldwide. Efforts have involved sharing information, coordinating search activities, and pooling resources to enhance the effectiveness of the search missions. The shared commitment to unraveling the mystery has transcended boundaries and united individuals with a common goal.

# VANISHED SKIES: THE MYSTERIOUS DISAPPEARANCE OF AMELIA EARHART

Despite decades of search missions, the mystery surrounding Amelia Earhart's disappearance remains unsolved. The extensive efforts expended to locate her aircraft, unravel the circumstances of her disappearance, and provide closure to her story reflect the enduring fascination and determination to find answers. The search for Amelia Earhart continues to evolve, fueled by advancements in technology, the dedication of researchers, and the hope that one day the truth will emerge from the depths of the Pacific Ocean.

The extensive search missions conducted in the aftermath of Amelia Earhart's disappearance have showcased the tenacity and dedication of individuals and organizations in their quest for answers. From initial search and rescue efforts to contemporary expeditions and scientific investigations, the search for Amelia Earhart has spanned decades, employing a wide array of techniques and technologies. While the mystery remains unresolved, the collective efforts of these missions have brought us closer to understanding the fate of one of aviation's most iconic figures. The search continues, driven by the enduring quest to uncover the truth and provide closure to the mystery that surrounds Amelia Earhart's ill-fated flight.

The search for Amelia Earhart and her aircraft has been marked by numerous challenges and obstacles. In this chapter, we analyze the difficulties encountered in locating Amelia Earhart, highlighting the complex nature of the search and the factors that have made the task of finding her and unraveling the mystery so challenging.

One of the foremost challenges in locating Amelia Earhart stems from the vastness of the Pacific Ocean. The area she traversed during her ill-fated flight is vast and covers millions of square miles. The sheer expanse of water presents a significant hurdle for search missions, as locating a small aircraft or wreckage within such a vast area is akin to finding a needle in a haystack.

Another challenge lies in the lack of specific crash site information. While the intended destination of Howland Island is known, the exact location where Amelia's aircraft may have gone down remains uncertain. The absence of precise data regarding her flight path, altitude, and potential deviations makes the search more challenging, as it requires extensive guesswork and exploration of multiple possibilities.

Amelia's flight path took her across remote and uninhabited regions of the Pacific Ocean, which adds to the difficulties in locating her and the aircraft. These areas often lack infrastructure and resources necessary for conducting extensive search operations. Remote islands and atolls may have rugged terrain, dense vegetation, and limited accessibility, making it arduous to conduct thorough searches on land.

In the event that Amelia's aircraft went down in the ocean, the search effort faces additional challenges due to the depth and complexity of underwater exploration. The depths of the Pacific Ocean can exceed several thousand meters, necessitating advanced equipment and expertise for conducting detailed searches. Factors such as strong currents, murky waters, and complex underwater topography make the task even more daunting.

The search for Amelia Earhart immediately following her disappearance was hampered by the limited technological advancements of the era. Sonar technology and other advanced equipment that are now available were not accessible at that time. This limited the effectiveness of search efforts and hindered the ability to locate potential wreckage or debris.

The passage of time has further complicated the search for Amelia Earhart. Over eight decades have elapsed since her disappearance, eroding physical evidence and increasing the challenges of locating any remaining remnants of the aircraft. Natural processes such as corrosion, deterioration, and sedimentation may have further concealed or damaged potential clues, impeding search missions in recent years.

The existence of multiple theories regarding Amelia Earhart's disappearance has led to search efforts being spread across various locations. The divergent hypotheses and speculative leads have dispersed resources and made it challenging to focus search missions effectively. Each theory requires its own exploration, diverting attention and resources from alternative areas of investigation.

The search for Amelia Earhart has faced numerous challenges, from the vastness of the Pacific Ocean to the lack of specific crash site information and the remote and uninhabited nature of the regions she traversed. The complexities of underwater exploration, limited technological advancements at the time, the passage of time, and the existence of multiple theories have further compounded the difficulties in locating her and her aircraft. Despite these challenges, the determination to unravel the mystery persists, as advancements in technology and collaboration continue to provide hope for potential breakthroughs in the future. The challenges faced in locating Amelia Earhart serve as a reminder of the complexity and enduring nature of one of aviation's greatest unsolved mysteries.

# VANISHED SKIES: THE MYSTERIOUS DISAPPEARANCE OF AMELIA EARHART

# Chapter 10: Theories and Speculations: What Happened?

The disappearance of Amelia Earhart has given rise to numerous hypotheses and theories attempting to explain the mystery surrounding her fate. In this chapter, we explore some of the prominent hypotheses that have emerged over the years, offering distinct perspectives on the enigma that surrounds Amelia Earhart.

## Hypothesis 1: Crash and Sinking at Sea:

One widely debated hypothesis suggests that Amelia Earhart's plane crashed into the Pacific Ocean, leading to her and Fred Noonan's demise at sea. This theory posits that navigation errors, fuel exhaustion, or adverse weather conditions may have caused a forced landing on the water, resulting in the aircraft sinking without leaving a trace.

## Hypothesis 2: Nikumaroro Island (Gardner Island):

An alternative hypothesis proposes that Amelia and Fred made a crash landing on Nikumaroro Island, now part of the Republic of Kiribati. Proponents of this theory argue that they survived the initial landing but eventually succumbed to the harsh environment and lack of resources. Search missions and archaeological investigations have been conducted on the island in an attempt to find evidence supporting this hypothesis.

**Hypothesis 3: Capture by the Japanese:**

Another hypothesis suggests that Amelia Earhart and Fred Noonan were captured by the Japanese government after landing in the Marshall Islands, which were under Japanese control at the time. This theory proposes that they were taken into custody, potentially as spies, and died in captivity. Some believe that the US government had knowledge of their fate but chose to cover it up.

**Hypothesis 4: Gardner Island (Now Nikumaroro) Castaway:**

Building upon the Nikumaroro Island theory, some researchers speculate that Amelia Earhart may have survived the crash landing and became a castaway on the island. This hypothesis suggests that she lived there for a period before ultimately perishing due to exposure, starvation, or other factors. Search missions have focused on finding physical evidence or artifacts supporting this hypothesis.

**Hypothesis 5: Technical Failure and Forced Landing on Uninhabited Island:**

According to this hypothesis, technical failures such as engine malfunctions or navigational instrument issues may have led to a forced landing on an unknown or uncharted island. Proponents of this theory suggest that Amelia and Fred survived the landing but were unable to attract attention or escape due to their remote location. The lack of radio communications and the subsequent disappearance of the aircraft would be attributed to the eventual destruction of the plane.

## Hypothesis 6: Espionage and Secret Mission:

An intriguing theory proposes that Amelia Earhart's circumnavigation attempt was a cover for a secret spy mission on behalf of the US government. According to this hypothesis, her disappearance was a result of her involvement in espionage activities. Supporters of this theory argue that her flight route and communication difficulties were intentional, aimed at covert operations rather than a genuine circumnavigation.

## Hypothesis 7: Lost in the Pacific, Never Found:

One sobering hypothesis posits that Amelia Earhart and Fred Noonan simply became lost over the vast expanse of the Pacific Ocean, and their remains and the wreckage of the aircraft were never located. This theory suggests that they may have flown off course, encountered adverse weather conditions, or experienced navigational challenges that led to their disappearance, leaving no definitive trace.

The various hypotheses surrounding Amelia Earhart's disappearance reflect the enduring mystery and intrigue surrounding her fate. From the possibilities of a crash and sinking at sea to landing on remote islands, capture by the Japanese, or involvement in espionage, each hypothesis offers a distinct narrative to explain the enigma. While extensive search efforts have been conducted, concrete evidence to support any particular hypothesis has yet to emerge. The enduring fascination with Amelia Earhart's disappearance continues to inspire researchers, investigators, and aviation enthusiasts to seek the truth, fueled by the hope that one day the puzzle will be solved, and the fate of one of aviation's most iconic figures will be unveiled.

Amelia Earhart's disappearance has been subject to extensive analysis by experts, investigators, and researchers. In this chapter, we delve into the evidence and expert opinions surrounding her disappearance, examining the various perspectives that have emerged in the ongoing quest to unravel the mystery of Amelia Earhart.

Eyewitness accounts have provided some insights into Amelia Earhart's ill-fated flight. Individuals residing near her intended flight path, such as Gilbertese settlers in the Pacific and islanders in the Marshall Islands, have claimed to have witnessed an aircraft similar to Earhart's Lockheed Electra and even reported encounters with Amelia and Fred Noonan. However, the accuracy and reliability of these accounts have been questioned due to the passage of time and the potential for confusion or misinterpretation.

Radio transmissions and communications play a crucial role in understanding Amelia Earhart's final moments. The last known radio communications between Amelia and the USS Itasca, the US Coast Guard cutter stationed near Howland Island, provide valuable insights into the challenges she faced. Analysis of the radio signals, voice patterns, and the context of the messages has been conducted to glean information about her flight path and potential issues encountered during the journey.

# VANISHED SKIES: THE MYSTERIOUS DISAPPEARANCE OF AMELIA EARHART

Photographs taken before Earhart's disappearance and the examination of physical evidence have also contributed to the investigation. Comparison of pre-flight and post-flight photographs of Earhart's aircraft has been conducted to identify any discrepancies or modifications. Additionally, the analysis of potential wreckage, artifacts, or remnants found on islands or in the ocean has been undertaken to determine if they are related to Amelia Earhart's ill-fated flight. However, definitive links to Earhart or her aircraft have remained elusive.

Experts in various fields, including aviation, forensic science, anthropology, and oceanography, have provided valuable insights into Amelia Earhart's disappearance. Forensic analysis of bones, DNA studies, and anthropological research have been conducted to identify human remains or artifacts connected to her. Additionally, aviation and navigational experts have analyzed flight data, weather patterns, and historical records to gain a deeper understanding of the events leading to her disappearance. However, these expert opinions often present different interpretations and conclusions, contributing to ongoing debates.

Extensive research of historical documentation and archives has been conducted to gather information relevant to Amelia Earhart's disappearance. Examination of flight records, navigational charts, weather reports, and personal correspondence has been undertaken to reconstruct the circumstances surrounding her ill-fated flight. Archival research continues to uncover new information and shed light on the events leading up to her disappearance.

The evidence and expert opinions surrounding Amelia Earhart's disappearance present a complex and often conflicting picture. Eyewitness accounts, radio transmissions, photographs, physical evidence, expert analysis, and historical documentation have all contributed to our understanding of the events surrounding her ill-fated flight. However, the lack of definitive evidence and the existence of multiple theories and interpretations continue to fuel speculation and debates. The pursuit of truth and resolution remains ongoing as experts, investigators, and enthusiasts strive to unravel the enduring mystery of Amelia Earhart's disappearance and provide closure to one of aviation's greatest enigmas.

# VANISHED SKIES: THE MYSTERIOUS DISAPPEARANCE OF AMELIA EARHART

# Chapter 11: Surviving Castaway: The Gardner Island Connection

The hypothesis proposing that Amelia Earhart made a crash landing on Gardner Island, now known as Nikumaroro, has gained significant attention in the search for answers about her disappearance. In this chapter, we investigate the Gardner Island hypothesis, exploring the evidence, research, and analysis that support the possibility of Amelia Earhart landing on this remote Pacific island.

Gardner Island, located in the Republic of Kiribati, lies within the vicinity of Amelia Earhart's intended flight path. The hypothesis suggests that after missing her target, Howland Island, Earhart may have continued flying and eventually landed on the uninhabited Gardner Island due to navigational challenges, fuel exhaustion, or other factors.

In the years following Earhart's disappearance, search missions and expeditions discovered intriguing pieces of evidence on Gardner Island. In 1937, an aluminum panel and a sextant box were found on the island, leading to speculation that they could have originated from Earhart's aircraft. Additionally, records from a 1940 British colonial settlement survey reported the discovery of a partial skeleton and a woman's shoe on the island.

The International Group for Historic Aircraft Recovery (TIGHAR) has played a prominent role in researching the

Gardner Island hypothesis. TIGHAR has conducted multiple expeditions to Nikumaroro, employing advanced technology, archival research, and archaeological methods to search for evidence related to Earhart's landing. Their investigations have focused on analyzing artifacts, conducting underwater surveys, and examining the island's landscape.

The artifacts discovered on Gardner Island have been carefully examined to determine their potential connection to Amelia Earhart's aircraft. TIGHAR has compared the aluminum panel and sextant box found on the island with those known to be part of Earhart's Lockheed Electra. While some similarities have been identified, conclusive proof linking the artifacts directly to Earhart's aircraft remains elusive.

The unique geography and characteristics of Nikumaroro have added weight to the Gardner Island hypothesis. The island's flat coral surface and extensive reef systems have been cited as potential landing areas for Earhart's aircraft. Researchers have suggested that Earhart and her navigator, Fred Noonan, could have survived the landing and attempted to find shelter and sustenance on the island before succumbing to the harsh environment.

Forensic analysis and anthropological studies have been conducted on skeletal remains discovered on Nikumaroro. While initial examinations of the partial skeleton found in 1940 led to inconclusive results, subsequent analysis has shed new light on the possibility that the remains may belong to a female of European descent, potentially supporting the

Gardner Island hypothesis. However, further investigation and DNA analysis are required for conclusive identification.

Despite the attention given to the Gardner Island hypothesis, it has faced critiques and alternative explanations. Skeptics argue that the discovered artifacts and skeletal remains may not be directly linked to Amelia Earhart, citing the possibility of other previous visitors or colonial activities on the island that could account for the findings.

The hypothesis suggesting that Amelia Earhart landed on Gardner Island (Nikumaroro) presents a compelling narrative supported by discoveries, research, and investigations. The artifacts found on the island, combined with the unique geographic features and the possibility of skeletal remains matching the description of Earhart, have led many to consider Nikumaroro as a potential landing site. However, definitive evidence directly linking these discoveries to Amelia Earhart remains elusive, and alternative explanations and critiques continue to fuel debates and skepticism. As the search for answers continues, further research and analysis may shed more light on the Gardner Island hypothesis and its role in unraveling the enduring mystery of Amelia Earhart's disappearance.

The search for Amelia Earhart and her aircraft has yielded several discoveries and clues in the vicinity of her intended flight path. In this chapter, we study the findings that have been uncovered, shedding light on the potential evidence and hints that have emerged in the ongoing investigation of Amelia Earhart's disappearance.

One notable discovery is the Bevington Photo, found in the personal effects of Captain Harold Gatty, Earhart's navigator on a 1935 flight. This photo, believed to have been taken during a stopover in Papua New Guinea, depicts what some claim to be Earhart's Lockheed Electra in the background. However, the photo's authenticity and connection to her final flight remain debated among experts.

During Amelia Earhart's ill-fated flight, a series of radio signals and distress calls were transmitted from her aircraft. These messages, received by various radio operators and the USS Itasca, provide crucial clues to her location and the challenges she faced. Analysis of these radio transmissions has offered insights into Earhart's flight path, communication difficulties, and potential navigational errors.

On the southeastern side of Nikumaroro Island (formerly Gardner Island), wreckage from the Norwich City, a British freighter that ran aground in 1929, was discovered during search expeditions. The presence of this wreckage in the vicinity has prompted researchers to consider whether Earhart's aircraft may have encountered a similar fate in the area.

In 1991, the International Group for Historic Aircraft Recovery (TIGHAR) conducted an expedition to Nikumaroro Island. During the expedition, a number of significant discoveries were made, including remnants of a campsite, a woman's shoe dating back to the 1930s, a bottle dating to the same period, and pieces of aluminum that may have come from Earhart's aircraft. These findings have fueled speculation that Earhart and Noonan may have survived the crash landing and attempted to live on the island before their eventual demise.

Sonar surveys and underwater explorations have been conducted in the vicinity of Howland Island and Nikumaroro Island to search for anomalies and potential wreckage. These surveys have identified seabed anomalies that could be associated with submerged debris or the remnants of Amelia Earhart's aircraft. However, further investigations are needed to confirm these findings.

Flotsam and jetsam, including items such as navigational equipment, aircraft debris, and personal effects, have been meticulously examined for any connection to Amelia Earhart and her aircraft. Researchers have scrutinized debris found on remote Pacific islands and coastlines, hoping to identify items that could be linked to Earhart's flight. While some artifacts have been discovered, their definitive association with Amelia Earhart remains elusive.

Forensic studies, including DNA analysis and bone examinations, have been conducted on skeletal remains found in the vicinity of Earhart's flight path. While initial assessments proved inconclusive, further research is ongoing to determine whether these remains belong to Amelia Earhart or her navigator, Fred Noonan. These studies hold the potential to provide definitive answers and closure to the enduring mystery.

The discoveries and clues found in the vicinity of Amelia Earhart's flight path have provided valuable insights into her ill-fated journey. The Bevington Photo, radio signals, the Norwich City wreckage, TIGHAR's expeditions, seabed anomalies, flotsam and jetsam, and ongoing forensic studies have all contributed to our understanding of the events surrounding her disappearance. While some findings offer tantalizing possibilities, definitive connections to Amelia Earhart and her aircraft have remained elusive. As the investigation continues and technology advances, there remains hope that further discoveries and analysis may bring us closer to unraveling the enigma and providing long-awaited answers to the mystery of Amelia Earhart's fate.

91

# Chapter 12: Controversies and Conspiracies

Amelia Earhart's disappearance has given rise to numerous conspiracy theories that attempt to explain the mystery surrounding her fate. In this chapter, we delve into some of the prominent conspiracy theories surrounding Amelia Earhart's disappearance, exploring the alternative narratives and speculation that have captivated the public imagination.

**Conspiracy Theory 1: Government Cover-Up:**

One prevalent conspiracy theory suggests that the United States government had knowledge of Amelia Earhart's fate but chose to cover it up. Proponents of this theory argue that Earhart's circumnavigation attempt was part of a government espionage mission, and her disappearance was intentionally orchestrated to hide her involvement in covert activities. Alleged motives for the cover-up range from protecting national security to concealing evidence of military operations.

**Conspiracy Theory 2: Capture by the Japanese:**

Another popular theory proposes that Amelia Earhart and Fred Noonan were captured by the Japanese military after crash-landing in the Marshall Islands. According to this theory, they were taken into custody as suspected spies, and their subsequent fate was concealed from the public. Proponents suggest that the US government was aware of their capture but refrained from intervening for political reasons.

## Conspiracy Theory 3: Living Under a New Identity:

A less conventional theory suggests that Amelia Earhart survived her flight and chose to disappear, assuming a new identity. Supporters argue that she orchestrated her own disappearance to escape the pressures of fame and public life. This theory speculates that she may have lived out her days under a different name, far removed from the public eye, for reasons unknown.

## Conspiracy Theory 4: Crash Landing on a Secret Island:

Some conspiracy theories propose that Amelia Earhart and Fred Noonan crash-landed on an undisclosed island intentionally chosen for its secrecy. Proponents argue that the US government orchestrated this landing to establish a hidden base for intelligence operations. According to this theory, Earhart and Noonan continued to work covertly for the government, unbeknownst to the public.

## Conspiracy Theory 5: Alien Abduction:

In the realm of more far-fetched theories, some speculate that Amelia Earhart's disappearance was the result of an alien abduction. Supporters of this theory propose that extraterrestrial beings intervened during her flight, abducting Earhart and Noonan for unknown purposes. This theory draws upon a belief in UFOs and alleged government collusion in concealing contact with extraterrestrial life.

**Conspiracy Theory 6: Time Travel:**

An outlandish theory suggests that Amelia Earhart's aircraft somehow fell victim to a time-travel phenomenon, transporting her and Noonan to another time or dimension. Proponents of this theory argue that Earhart's disappearance was not a conventional aviation incident but rather an inexplicable encounter with temporal anomalies.

Conspiracy theories surrounding Amelia Earhart's disappearance have proliferated over the years, offering alternative explanations to the enduring mystery. These theories range from government cover-ups and capture by the Japanese to living under a new identity, crash landing on secret islands, alien abduction, and even time travel. While intriguing to consider, these conspiracy theories often lack substantial evidence and rely on speculation and imagination. The search for the truth behind Amelia Earhart's disappearance remains grounded in the diligent investigation of facts, analysis of evidence, and examination of historical records. As researchers, investigators, and aviation enthusiasts continue their quest for answers, it is important to approach conspiracy theories with skepticism and prioritize verifiable evidence in the pursuit of unraveling one of aviation's greatest enigmas.

Claims of cover-ups and secret missions surrounding Amelia Earhart's disappearance have fueled speculation and intrigue for decades. In this chapter, we delve into the allegations of government involvement, espionage, and covert operations, examining the evidence and considerations surrounding these claims.

One of the primary claims suggests that the United States government was involved in covering up the true circumstances of Amelia Earhart's disappearance. Proponents argue that her flight was not a simple circumnavigation attempt but part of a covert operation sanctioned by the government. The alleged reasons for government involvement vary, including espionage, military reconnaissance, or even political motivations.

Some theories suggest that Amelia Earhart's flight was a cover for an espionage mission. Proponents argue that her disappearance was intentional, and she and Fred Noonan were collecting intelligence information during their journey. It is suggested that their aircraft was equipped with advanced surveillance technology or that they were gathering data on specific areas of interest to the US government.

Claims of covert military operations and involvement in Amelia Earhart's disappearance have also been put forth. Some theories propose that her flight path intersected with classified military activities, and her aircraft may have inadvertently stumbled upon sensitive operations. This theory suggests that the US government was keen on preventing the exposure of these activities, leading to a cover-up of Earhart's fate.

The motives attributed to potential government cover-ups vary widely. Supporters of these claims argue that national security concerns, geopolitical factors, or protecting classified information were primary reasons for concealing the truth about Earhart's disappearance. The government's desire to control public perception, avoid embarrassment, or maintain an advantage in international relations has also been posited as motivations for secrecy.

Critics of the cover-up claims point out the lack of concrete evidence to support these allegations. The absence of reliable eyewitness accounts, official documents, or whistleblower testimonies specific to Earhart's disappearance has led skeptics to question the validity of these claims. They argue that circumstantial evidence and speculation alone cannot substantiate the existence of cover-ups or secret missions.

Government agencies, including the United States Navy and the Federal Bureau of Investigation (FBI), have conducted investigations into Amelia Earhart's disappearance. Official statements and reports have consistently maintained that there is no evidence to support the claims of cover-ups or secret missions. These statements highlight the exhaustive search efforts, lack of conclusive findings, and the absence of any verifiable evidence pointing to government involvement.

While claims of cover-ups and secret missions surrounding Amelia Earhart's disappearance have captured the public imagination, the evidence supporting these allegations remains largely speculative. Critics argue that the absence of substantial evidence, official statements refuting these claims, and the lack of whistleblower revelations make it challenging to substantiate the existence of government cover-ups or covert operations. As the search for the truth continues, it is important to approach these claims with critical thinking and rely on verifiable evidence and official investigations to unravel the enduring mystery surrounding Amelia Earhart's fate.

# Chapter 13: Forensic Investigations and New Technologies

Advancements in modern forensic techniques have provided new avenues for investigating the disappearance of Amelia Earhart. In this chapter, we explore the application of these techniques to her case, discussing how they have contributed to the ongoing search for answers and the potential for uncovering the truth about her fate.

One significant advancement in forensic science is the application of DNA analysis. This technique can be utilized to examine skeletal remains, hair samples, or other biological materials discovered in the vicinity of Amelia Earhart's disappearance. By comparing the DNA profiles of these samples with known familial DNA, experts can potentially determine if the remains belong to Amelia Earhart or her navigator, Fred Noonan. DNA analysis offers a promising avenue for definitively identifying human remains and establishing a conclusive link to Earhart.

Stable isotope analysis is a technique used to analyze the chemical composition of skeletal remains or other organic materials. By examining the isotopic ratios of elements like oxygen, carbon, and nitrogen, researchers can gain insights into an individual's geographical origin and dietary habits. Applying stable isotope analysis to the remains found near Earhart's flight path could provide clues about their origin and potentially shed light on whether they are connected to her ill-fated journey.

Forensic anthropology plays a crucial role in examining skeletal remains and reconstructing the circumstances surrounding an individual's death. Forensic anthropologists study factors such as bone morphology, age estimation, trauma analysis, and the determination of sex and stature. Applying these techniques to skeletal remains found in the vicinity of Earhart's disappearance could help in establishing the identity of the remains and provide insights into the cause of death.

Digital forensics involves the examination of electronic devices, such as computers, cameras, or navigational equipment, to extract and analyze relevant data. In Amelia Earhart's case, digital forensics could be used to examine navigational records, flight logs, or any electronic communications that may have been captured during her ill-fated flight. Recovering and analyzing digital evidence could help reconstruct the flight path and provide valuable insights into the circumstances surrounding her disappearance.

Remote sensing techniques, including satellite imagery and aerial photography, combined with geospatial analysis, can aid in the search for physical evidence related to Amelia Earhart's disappearance. High-resolution imagery can be examined to identify potential wreckage, debris fields, or disturbed areas in remote locations. Geospatial analysis helps in mapping and visualizing data related to Earhart's flight path, potential landing sites, or areas of interest for search missions.

# VANISHED SKIES: THE MYSTERIOUS DISAPPEARANCE OF AMELIA EARHART

Sonar technology has advanced significantly, allowing for detailed underwater mapping and the identification of potential wreckage. By utilizing advanced sonar systems, researchers can scan the ocean floor in the vicinity of Earhart's intended flight path, searching for anomalies that may indicate the presence of her aircraft. Underwater exploration techniques, including remotely operated vehicles (ROVs) and submersibles, enable the investigation of potential crash sites or areas of interest at greater depths.

Modern forensic techniques have revolutionized the investigation into Amelia Earhart's disappearance. DNA analysis, stable isotope analysis, forensic anthropology, digital forensics, remote sensing, and underwater exploration provide new avenues for examining evidence, reconstructing events, and potentially identifying human remains. These advancements offer hope for resolving the enduring mystery and providing long-awaited answers to the fate of Amelia Earhart. As technology continues to advance, the application of modern forensic techniques will play a vital role in unraveling the enigma that surrounds one of aviation's greatest mysteries.

Recent years have witnessed exciting discoveries and technological advancements that have propelled the search for Amelia Earhart and shed new light on her disappearance. In this chapter, we highlight some of the notable findings and advancements that have revitalized the investigation, bringing renewed hope of unraveling the mystery surrounding Amelia Earhart.

State-of-the-art oceanographic surveys and high-resolution imaging technologies have enabled comprehensive mapping and exploration of the ocean floor in the vicinity of Amelia Earhart's intended flight path. These advanced sonar systems, side-scan sonar, and multibeam echo sounders provide detailed images and data of underwater topography, allowing researchers to identify potential wreckage or anomalies that may be linked to Earhart's aircraft.

The utilization of underwater robotic systems, such as remotely operated vehicles (ROVs) and autonomous underwater vehicles (AUVs), has significantly enhanced the search capabilities in deep-sea environments. These robotic systems can navigate and explore vast areas of the ocean floor with precision, capturing high-definition imagery and collecting samples for further analysis. Their deployment has expanded the scope of search missions, enabling more comprehensive investigations.

Advancements in DNA analysis techniques have provided enhanced capabilities for the identification and analysis of human remains. New methodologies and improvements in DNA extraction and sequencing have increased the likelihood of obtaining viable genetic material from skeletal remains found in the vicinity of Amelia Earhart's disappearance. These advancements offer the potential for more accurate identification and the possibility of establishing a definitive link to Earhart or her navigator, Fred Noonan.

The digitization of archives and the availability of historical records online have facilitated extensive research into Amelia

# VANISHED SKIES: THE MYSTERIOUS DISAPPEARANCE OF AMELIA EARHART

Earhart's journey and the events surrounding her disappearance. Researchers now have greater access to previously inaccessible documents, flight logs, correspondence, and other relevant materials. This digital access has opened up new avenues for analysis, allowing for more comprehensive investigations and the discovery of overlooked information.

Forensic anthropology continues to benefit from technological advancements. Cutting-edge imaging techniques, such as computed tomography (CT) scanning, three-dimensional (3D) modeling, and facial reconstruction software, enhance the examination and analysis of skeletal remains. These techniques provide more detailed insights into bone morphology, trauma analysis, and the potential reconstruction of facial features, aiding in the identification and understanding of recovered remains.

The availability of high-resolution satellite imagery and the application of artificial intelligence (AI) algorithms have improved the efficiency and accuracy of search efforts. Satellite imagery can be analyzed using AI algorithms to detect potential wreckage, disturbed areas, or signs of human activity on remote islands or coastlines. This combination of satellite imagery and AI technology accelerates the identification and prioritization of search areas, increasing the chances of uncovering significant clues.

In recent years, collaborative research efforts and data sharing among different organizations and institutions have expanded, promoting a more coordinated approach to the search for Amelia Earhart. Experts, researchers, and organizations worldwide are pooling their resources, expertise, and data to tackle the mystery collectively. Collaborative initiatives foster the exchange of knowledge, accelerate progress, and bring diverse perspectives to the investigation.

Recent discoveries and technological advancements have injected new energy and optimism into the search for Amelia Earhart. From advanced oceanographic surveys and underwater robotics to DNA analysis, archival research, and AI-assisted satellite imagery, these developments have expanded our capabilities, improved search efforts, and enhanced forensic analysis. As technology continues to evolve and collaborative research efforts persist, the possibility of uncovering the truth about Amelia Earhart's disappearance grows closer. These recent discoveries and advancements provide renewed hope that the enduring mystery will be solved, bringing closure to one of aviation's most captivating enigmas.

# VANISHED SKIES: THE MYSTERIOUS DISAPPEARANCE OF AMELIA EARHART

# Chapter 14: Amelia's Legacy: Inspiring Future Aviators

Amelia Earhart's legacy extends far beyond her remarkable accomplishments as an aviator. She has left an indelible mark on the history of women in aviation, inspiring generations of women to pursue their dreams and break barriers in a traditionally male-dominated field. In this chapter, we explore Earhart's enduring influence and the impact she has had on women in aviation.

Amelia Earhart shattered societal expectations and defied gender norms of her time by entering the world of aviation. In an era when flying was predominantly seen as a male pursuit, Earhart fearlessly pursued her passion, demonstrating that women could excel in the field and compete on equal footing with their male counterparts. Her courage and determination paved the way for future generations of women to pursue their dreams and challenge societal stereotypes.

Earhart's achievements inspired countless women to take an interest in aviation. Through her achievements and public visibility, she encouraged women to consider aviation as a viable career path and ignited a sense of possibility and adventure in their minds. Many women who followed in her footsteps credit Earhart for inspiring them to pursue careers as pilots, engineers, astronauts, and aviation professionals.

Earhart was a staunch advocate for women in aviation and worked tirelessly to promote their participation in the field. She co-founded The Ninety-Nines, an international organization of women pilots, with the goal of providing camaraderie, support, and opportunities for women aviators. The organization continues to thrive today, providing a network of support for women in aviation and honoring Earhart's vision of empowering female pilots.

Amelia Earhart's pioneering spirit inspired a new generation of female aviators who became trailblazers in their own right. Women such as Jacqueline Cochran, the first woman to break the sound barrier, and Sally Ride, the first American woman in space, were among those influenced by Earhart's courage and determination. Earhart's legacy has empowered women to challenge limits, break records, and achieve remarkable feats in aviation and space exploration.

Earhart's influence extends beyond inspiring women to pursue aviation careers. Her accomplishments brought attention to the need for gender equality in the industry. By challenging gender barriers and advocating for women's involvement in aviation, Earhart contributed to the ongoing progress toward gender equality in both the cockpit and the boardroom. Her legacy serves as a reminder of the importance of inclusion and diversity in the aviation industry.

Amelia Earhart's enduring influence can be seen in the countless women who have followed in her footsteps, making significant contributions to the field of aviation. Today, women serve as pilots, astronauts, engineers, air traffic controllers, and leaders in aviation organizations. Earhart's legacy continues to inspire women to overcome obstacles, pursue their passions, and make their mark in an industry that she helped shape.

Amelia Earhart's impact on women in aviation is immeasurable. Her trailblazing spirit, determination, and advocacy for women's involvement in aviation have opened doors and shattered glass ceilings. Earhart's enduring influence continues to inspire women to dream big, pursue careers in aviation, and break barriers in a field historically dominated by men. Her legacy serves as a powerful reminder that with courage, determination, and unwavering belief in oneself, anything is possible. Amelia Earhart will forever be celebrated as an icon and a champion for gender equality in aviation.

Amelia Earhart's impact extends beyond the realm of aviation. Her remarkable achievements and charismatic personality have had a profound influence on society and popular culture. In this chapter, we explore Earhart's lasting impact, examining how she became an enduring symbol of courage, adventure, and empowerment.

Amelia Earhart emerged as an icon of female empowerment during a time when women's roles were often confined to traditional domestic spheres. Her determination to pursue her passion for aviation and her trailblazing achievements challenged societal norms and inspired women around the world. Earhart's spirit of fearlessness and resilience made her a symbol of women's capability, independence, and the potential for greatness.

Earhart's extraordinary feats of aviation captured the imagination of people worldwide and inspired a generation of adventurers and explorers. Her solo transatlantic flight, attempted circumnavigation, and willingness to push the boundaries of what was considered possible sparked a sense of adventure and curiosity in countless individuals. Many sought to follow in her footsteps, embarking on their own daring journeys and explorations.

Amelia Earhart played a significant role in promoting aviation and air travel. Her high-profile status and record-breaking achievements brought attention to the field of aviation, making it more accessible and appealing to the general public. Earhart's passion for flying and her ability to capture the public's imagination helped popularize aviation and pave the way for the growth of commercial air travel.

Earhart's courage and determination in the face of challenges and adversity made her an enduring symbol of resilience. Her relentless pursuit of her goals, despite numerous setbacks and risks, resonated with people of all backgrounds. Earhart's unwavering spirit continues to inspire individuals to overcome obstacles, embrace their dreams, and persevere in the face of adversity.

Amelia Earhart's life and disappearance have been the subject of numerous books, films, and documentaries. These portrayals have further cemented her status as a cultural icon and ensured that her story remains a part of popular culture. Whether in biographies, fictionalized accounts, or dramatizations,

Earhart's character and legacy continue to captivate audiences and keep her memory alive.

Amelia Earhart's fashion choices, characterized by her iconic leather bomber jacket, goggles, and aviator caps, have influenced popular style trends. Her distinctive attire has become synonymous with aviation and adventure, inspiring fashion designers and influencing the aesthetics of both casual and high fashion. Earhart's timeless style continues to be celebrated and replicated in various forms of popular culture.

Amelia Earhart's impact extends to the realm of feminism and gender equality. Her achievements in a male-dominated field challenged gender stereotypes and helped pave the way for future generations of women. Earhart's legacy continues to inspire ongoing discussions about gender equality, empowering women to pursue their passions, break barriers, and strive for equal opportunities in all aspects of life.

Amelia Earhart's impact on society and popular culture is far-reaching and enduring. As an icon of female empowerment, she has inspired generations of individuals to embrace their dreams, challenge societal norms, and pursue adventure. Earhart's influence extends beyond aviation, encompassing fashion, literature, film, and the ongoing struggle for gender equality. Her legacy continues to resonate, reminding us of the power of courage, determination, and the pursuit of one's passions. Amelia Earhart's spirit lives on as a symbol of empowerment and a testament to the enduring impact of those who dare to dream and defy limitations.

# Chapter 15: Earhart's Life in Retrospect

A melia Earhart's life was one filled with extraordinary accomplishments and lasting contributions. As we conclude our journey through her awe-inspiring story, it is essential to reflect on her significant achievements and the ways in which she has left an indelible mark on history.

Amelia Earhart's pioneering spirit propelled her to become one of the most celebrated figures in aviation history. She shattered gender barriers and inspired countless women to pursue their dreams in the field of aviation. Her courage, determination, and unwavering belief in herself paved the way for future generations of female aviators.

Earhart's record-breaking flights showcased her exceptional skill and tenacity. Her solo transatlantic flight, becoming the first woman to achieve such a feat, solidified her place in the annals of aviation history. Additionally, her attempted circumnavigation of the globe demonstrated her daring spirit and ambition to conquer new frontiers.

Amelia Earhart was not only a trailblazer but also a fierce advocate for women's participation in aviation. Through co-founding The Ninety-Nines, she created a platform for female pilots to connect, support each other, and further the cause of gender equality in the aviation industry. Her advocacy work continues to inspire women in aviation to this day.

Earhart's adventurous spirit and unwavering determination have made her an enduring symbol of courage. Her willingness to push the boundaries, explore new horizons, and embrace the unknown captivated the public's imagination. Earhart's legacy encourages individuals to step outside their comfort zones, take risks, and pursue their passions fearlessly.

Amelia Earhart's contributions extend beyond her own time. Her influence has transcended generations, inspiring countless individuals to dream big and defy limitations. She has ignited a sense of possibility and adventure in the hearts and minds of people worldwide. Earhart's legacy lives on in the countless aviators, explorers, and trailblazers who continue to be inspired by her remarkable life.

Amelia Earhart's impact on popular culture is undeniable. Her iconic image, adventurous spirit, and legacy have been celebrated in literature, film, fashion, and art. Her story continues to captivate audiences and serves as a reminder of the power of determination, resilience, and breaking barriers. Earhart's name has become synonymous with courage and empowerment.

Amelia Earhart's journey challenged societal expectations and paved the way for greater gender equality. By fearlessly entering the male-dominated field of aviation, she shattered stereotypes and demonstrated the capabilities of women in traditionally male spheres. Earhart's accomplishments sparked discussions and advancements in the ongoing pursuit of gender equality.

# VANISHED SKIES: THE MYSTERIOUS DISAPPEARANCE OF AMELIA EARHART

Amelia Earhart's accomplishments and contributions to aviation, gender equality, and popular culture are undeniably profound. Her legacy as an aviation pioneer, record-breaker, advocate, and symbol of courage continues to inspire individuals to pursue their dreams and challenge societal limitations. Earhart's enduring impact serves as a testament to the indomitable human spirit and the ability to leave a lasting imprint on the world. As we reflect on her remarkable journey, we celebrate Amelia Earhart as an icon, a trailblazer, and an inspiration for generations to come.

Amelia Earhart's impact on the aviation industry is profound and far-reaching. Her pioneering spirit, record-breaking flights, and advocacy for women in aviation have left an indelible mark. In this chapter, we analyze her lasting legacy in the aviation industry and explore how her contributions continue to shape and inspire the field.

Amelia Earhart's remarkable achievements continue to inspire women to pursue careers in aviation. She shattered gender barriers, proving that women are equally capable of excelling in the field. Her legacy serves as a constant reminder that determination, skill, and passion are not limited by gender, encouraging women to enter aviation and contribute to its advancement.

Earhart's unwavering commitment to gender equality in aviation laid the foundation for significant progress in the industry. By advocating for women pilots and co-founding The Ninety-Nines, she paved the way for increased opportunities and recognition for women in aviation. Her legacy continues to drive efforts towards equal representation and opportunities for all genders in the industry.

Amelia Earhart's adventurous spirit and willingness to explore new frontiers have inspired generations of aviators and adventurers. Her solo transatlantic flight and attempted circumnavigation of the globe embody the spirit of exploration and the desire to push the boundaries of what is deemed possible. Earhart's legacy encourages aviators to embrace adventure, discovery, and the pursuit of new horizons.

Earhart's impact extends beyond her personal achievements. Her record-breaking flights and involvement in aviation propelled advancements in aircraft design, navigation systems, and safety protocols. Her experiences and insights as a pilot contributed to the ongoing improvement of aviation technology, enhancing the safety and efficiency of air travel for all.

Amelia Earhart's dedication to aviation education has had a lasting impact on the industry. Through scholarships and educational initiatives, her legacy continues to support aspiring pilots and aviation professionals. These programs foster the development of new talent, ensuring a bright future for aviation and cultivating a diverse and skilled workforce.

Amelia Earhart's legacy transcends time, inspiring future generations of aviators. Her tenacity, courage, and pioneering spirit serve as a constant reminder that dreams can be achieved through determination and perseverance. Earhart's story continues to motivate individuals to overcome obstacles, embrace their passions, and strive for excellence in the aviation industry.

Amelia Earhart has become a symbol of adventure and courage, representing the spirit of exploration and the pursuit of dreams. Her name evokes images of daring flights, bold ambitions, and fearlessness in the face of challenges. As a cultural icon, Earhart's legacy captures the imagination of people worldwide, perpetuating a sense of awe and admiration for her contributions to aviation.

Amelia Earhart's lasting legacy in the aviation industry is multifaceted and profound. Her influence is evident in the increasing representation of women in aviation, advancements in aviation technology, and the promotion of gender equality. Earhart's remarkable accomplishments, advocacy work, and adventurous spirit continue to inspire current and future generations of aviators. Her legacy serves as a beacon of courage, determination, and the pursuit of excellence, shaping the aviation industry and inspiring individuals to reach for the skies. Amelia Earhart's impact will endure, ensuring that her contributions to aviation will always be remembered and celebrated.

# Chapter 16: Unraveling the Mystery: Latest Developments

Breakthroughs and discoveries in the search for answers regarding Amelia Earhart's disappearance have been ongoing since her ill-fated flight in 1937. While no definitive answers have been found, several noteworthy breakthroughs and discoveries have emerged over the years. Here are some key developments:

## 1. TIGHAR's Nikumaroro Hypothesis:

The International Group for Historic Aircraft Recovery (TIGHAR) has conducted extensive research and expeditions to Nikumaroro, formerly known as Gardner Island, in the Pacific. They have proposed a hypothesis that Earhart and Noonan made a controlled landing on the island and survived as castaways for a period of time. TIGHAR has discovered potential artifacts, including pieces of a woman's shoe, a pocket knife, and a navigational tool, which are believed to have belonged to Earhart. While inconclusive, these discoveries have fueled further interest and investigation into the Nikumaroro hypothesis.

## 2. Forensic Analysis of Bones:

In 1940, a British expedition on Nikumaroro discovered skeletal remains on the island. The bones were initially believed to belong to a male, but recent forensic analysis has challenged this conclusion. In 1998, TIGHAR reexamined the measurements and found that they could indeed match Earhart's physical proportions. However, the bones themselves have since been lost, preventing further analysis and conclusive identification.

### 3. Enhanced Imaging Technology:

Advancements in imaging technology have been crucial in the search for wreckage and clues. High-resolution satellite imagery, sonar systems, and underwater exploration have been utilized to survey the ocean floor and remote areas of interest. These technologies have helped in identifying anomalies, potential debris fields, and disturbed areas that could indicate the presence of Earhart's aircraft or artifacts related to her disappearance.

### 4. Historical Records and Archival Research:

Continued efforts to uncover and analyze historical records, flight logs, navigational charts, and personal correspondence have provided valuable insights into Earhart's flight and possible locations of interest. Researchers have delved into archives, libraries, and private collections to piece together information that may shed light on the circumstances surrounding her disappearance.

### 5. Collaboration and Interdisciplinary Research:

Collaboration among experts from various fields, including aviation history, archaeology, forensics, and oceanography, has been instrumental in advancing the search for answers. By combining expertise, resources, and data, researchers have been able to approach the mystery from multiple angles, enriching the investigation and increasing the likelihood of breakthroughs.

It is important to note that despite these breakthroughs and discoveries, the mystery surrounding Amelia Earhart's disappearance remains unsolved. The search for definitive answers continues, fueled by ongoing advancements in technology, persistent exploration of potential sites, and the dedication of researchers and organizations committed to unraveling the enigma that surrounds one of aviation's most enduring mysteries.

Ongoing efforts to solve the mystery of Amelia Earhart's disappearance have persisted for decades. Numerous organizations, researchers, and individuals continue to explore different avenues, utilize advanced technology, and employ collaborative approaches to uncover the truth. Despite the dedication and ongoing efforts of those involved, the mystery surrounding Amelia Earhart's disappearance remains unsolved. However, these ongoing endeavors in research, exploration, collaboration, and technological advancements keep the search alive. The collective goal is to uncover the truth, bring closure to the mystery, and honor the enduring legacy of Amelia Earhart.

# Chapter 17: The Earhart Project: Expedition and Research

Prominent expeditions and research initiatives dedicated to finding answers about Amelia Earhart's disappearance have been conducted by various organizations and researchers over the years. These efforts have involved extensive fieldwork, technological advancements, and collaborative approaches. Here are some notable expeditions and initiatives:

## 1. Earhart Project by TIGHAR:

The International Group for Historic Aircraft Recovery (TIGHAR) has been at the forefront of research and expeditions related to Earhart's disappearance. Since 1988, TIGHAR has conducted multiple expeditions to Nikumaroro (formerly known as Gardner Island) in the Pacific. These expeditions involve archaeological surveys, underwater searches, and the analysis of potential artifacts. TIGHAR's Earhart Project has brought attention to the hypothesis that Earhart made a controlled landing on Nikumaroro and survived as a castaway.

## 2. The Niku VII Expedition:

In 2019, TIGHAR organized the Niku VII Expedition to Nikumaroro, focusing on surveying and documenting specific locations on the island. The expedition utilized advanced technology, including remote-controlled underwater vehicles, to search for potential wreckage and artifacts related to Earhart's disappearance. While the expedition did not yield definitive evidence, it contributed to the ongoing understanding of the island's history and potential connections to Earhart.

### 3. Project Blue Angel:

Initiated in 1991 by Richard E. Gillespie and TIGHAR, Project Blue Angel aimed to investigate the hypothesis that Earhart's Lockheed Electra 10E crashed and sank in the waters off Howland Island. The project involved extensive sonar searches and imaging of the ocean floor in the vicinity of Howland Island. Although no conclusive evidence was found, the project contributed valuable data and insights into the search area.

### 4. The Amelia Earhart Search LLC:

The Amelia Earhart Search LLC, led by Robert Ballard, renowned oceanographer and discoverer of the RMS Titanic wreck, embarked on an expedition in 2019 to search for Earhart's Lockheed Electra at a potential crash site near Howland Island. Utilizing state-of-the-art underwater technology, including remotely operated vehicles (ROVs) and advanced sonar systems, the expedition aimed to locate and identify the wreckage. However, the search did not yield definitive results.

### 5. The Earhart Project at Purdue University:

# VANISHED SKIES: THE MYSTERIOUS DISAPPEARANCE OF AMELIA EARHART

Purdue University, Amelia Earhart's alma mater, has been involved in ongoing research and analysis related to her disappearance. The university houses a vast collection of Earhart's personal papers and archives, which have been a valuable resource for researchers. The Earhart Project at Purdue University focuses on analyzing historical documents, flight logs, and artifacts to contribute to the understanding of Earhart's final flight and potential theories.

These prominent expeditions and research initiatives highlight the dedication of organizations, researchers, and individuals in unraveling the mystery surrounding Amelia Earhart's disappearance. While definitive answers have not yet been found, these efforts have contributed to the body of knowledge, deepened our understanding of the circumstances, and generated new leads and theories. The ongoing search remains a testament to the enduring fascination and commitment to finding answers about one of aviation's most enduring mysteries.

The search for answers regarding Amelia Earhart's disappearance has relied on various technologies and methodologies to explore potential crash sites, survey remote areas, and analyze historical data. Here are some of the technologies and methodologies employed in these endeavors:

## 1. Sonar Systems and Bathymetry:

Sonar systems, including side-scan sonar and multibeam echo sounders, have been instrumental in mapping the ocean floor and identifying potential wreckage sites. These systems emit sound waves and measure their reflection to create detailed images of the seafloor. Bathymetric data, derived from sonar measurements, provide valuable information about underwater topography and potential crash sites.

## 2. Remote Sensing and Satellite Imagery:

Advanced remote sensing technologies, such as high-resolution satellite imagery and aerial surveys, have been employed to identify potential crash sites, disturbed areas, or signs of human activity. These images provide detailed visual data, allowing researchers to examine large areas for anomalies, wreckage, or other clues related to Earhart's disappearance.

## 3. Underwater Robotics:

Remotely operated vehicles (ROVs) and autonomous underwater vehicles (AUVs) have been used in underwater explorations and surveys. These robotic systems are equipped with cameras, sensors, and manipulator arms, enabling researchers to conduct detailed investigations of potential crash sites, retrieve samples, and capture high-resolution imagery of underwater environments that are otherwise inaccessible to humans.

## 4. LiDAR (Light Detection and Ranging):

LiDAR technology uses laser pulses to measure distances and create highly accurate three-dimensional representations of terrain and objects. It has been employed in aerial surveys and archaeological investigations to reveal hidden features or structures that may be relevant to Earhart's disappearance.

LiDAR data can help uncover anomalies, identify potential wreckage, or aid in the identification of significant geological or archaeological features.

## 5. Forensic Anthropology and DNA Analysis:

Forensic anthropological techniques have been employed to analyze recovered skeletal remains and assess their potential connection to Earhart. These methods include the examination of bone morphology, trauma analysis, and the reconstruction of facial features. Additionally, advancements in DNA analysis have opened up possibilities for identifying remains and establishing genetic connections, potentially offering definitive answers regarding the identity of discovered remains.

## 6. Historical Research and Archival Analysis:

Extensive research and analysis of historical records, flight logs, navigational charts, and personal correspondence have been essential in reconstructing the events surrounding Earhart's final flight. Scholars and researchers have delved into archives, libraries, and personal collections to gather information, examine primary sources, and uncover overlooked details that may contribute to the understanding of Earhart's disappearance.

## 7. Collaboration and Interdisciplinary Approaches:

Collaboration among experts from various fields, such as aviation history, archaeology, oceanography, and forensics, has been a hallmark of the ongoing search. Interdisciplinary approaches allow for the integration of diverse perspectives, knowledge, and methodologies, enhancing the search efforts and increasing the likelihood of breakthroughs.

These technologies and methodologies, combined with the expertise and dedication of researchers, continue to shape the search for answers regarding Amelia Earhart's disappearance. While the mystery remains unsolved, the application of these advanced tools and methods provides hope for future discoveries and a potential resolution to one of aviation's most enduring enigmas.

# VANISHED SKIES: THE MYSTERIOUS DISAPPEARANCE OF AMELIA EARHART

129

# Chapter 18: Eyewitness Accounts and Testimonies

Eyewitness testimonies related to Amelia Earhart's disappearance have played a significant role in attempting to reconstruct the events surrounding her final flight. While eyewitness accounts can vary in reliability and consistency, they offer valuable perspectives and insights. Here are some notable eyewitness testimonies that have been collected and analyzed:

## 1. Eyewitnesses on Howland Island:

Howland Island, the intended destination of Earhart and Fred Noonan, had personnel stationed there during the search and rescue efforts. Eyewitnesses on the island reported their observations and interactions with radio operators during the critical time when Earhart and Noonan were attempting to locate the island. These testimonies provide valuable information about the communications and weather conditions at the time.

## 2. Itasca Radio Operators:

The crew members and radio operators on the US Coast Guard cutter Itasca, stationed near Howland Island to provide navigational assistance, provided their accounts of their attempts to establish radio contact with Earhart. These testimonies shed light on the communication challenges faced and the possible interpretation of Earhart's transmissions.

## 3. Witnesses on Gardner Island (Nikumaroro):

During subsequent expeditions to Nikumaroro (formerly Gardner Island), eyewitness testimonies were collected from local inhabitants and British colonial officials who were present on the island after Earhart's disappearance. These testimonies provide insights into potential sightings of aircraft wreckage, distress signals, and signs of human activity that could be linked to Earhart and Noonan.

## 4. Pacific Islanders:

Inhabitants of various Pacific islands, including the Marshall Islands and the Gilbert Islands, have claimed to have witnessed the crash or the presence of Earhart and Noonan in the area. These accounts vary in credibility and consistency, and their veracity is subject to further investigation and analysis.

## 5. Earhart's Final Takeoff Witnesses:

Individuals who were present at Lae, Papua New Guinea, where Earhart's final takeoff occurred, have provided testimonies regarding the aircraft's departure, its condition, and the weather conditions at the time. These accounts contribute to the understanding of the initial stages of the ill-fated flight.

## 6. Post-Disappearance Sightings:

# VANISHED SKIES: THE MYSTERIOUS DISAPPEARANCE OF AMELIA EARHART

Numerous sightings of an aircraft resembling Earhart's Lockheed Electra were reported in the years following her disappearance. Witnesses from various locations, such as the Marshall Islands, Saipan, and even the United States, claimed to have seen an aircraft or individuals matching Earhart's description. These testimonies have sparked interest and speculation, although their credibility remains a subject of scrutiny and analysis.

Analyzing eyewitness testimonies requires careful evaluation, cross-referencing, and corroborating evidence. Discrepancies, inconsistencies, and the passage of time can affect the reliability of such testimonies. Researchers and investigators have employed techniques, including forensic analysis, comparative assessments, and the evaluation of corroborating evidence, to assess the credibility and relevance of eyewitness accounts.

It is essential to note that while eyewitness testimonies provide valuable insights, they alone may not provide conclusive evidence about the circumstances of Earhart's disappearance. To unravel the mystery, a comprehensive approach that combines various lines of evidence, including physical artifacts, forensic analysis, historical research, and technological advancements, is necessary.

Evaluating the credibility and relevance of eyewitness testimonies related to Amelia Earhart's disappearance is a critical aspect of the investigation. Each testimony must be carefully scrutinized to assess its reliability, consistency, corroboration, and potential biases. Here are some factors considered in evaluating the credibility and relevance of eyewitness testimonies:

## 1. Proximity and Direct Observation:

Eyewitnesses who were in close proximity to the events and had direct observation of the circumstances surrounding Earhart's disappearance generally carry more weight in terms of credibility. Their testimonies are more likely to provide accurate and firsthand accounts of what transpired. Testimonies from individuals who were in the vicinity of Earhart's final takeoff, on Howland Island, or in the immediate aftermath of her disappearance are particularly significant.

## 2. Corroboration and Consistency:

Eyewitness testimonies that are consistent with each other, as well as with other available evidence and records, are more likely to be deemed credible. Multiple independent witnesses corroborating similar details, without prior knowledge of each other's accounts, lend greater credibility to their testimonies. Consistency in the core elements of their narratives, such as the timing, location, and key events, strengthens the reliability of their claims.

## 3. Expert Analysis and Forensic Examination:

Expert analysis and forensic examination can be employed to assess the credibility and relevance of eyewitness testimonies. Forensic experts, historians, and investigators scrutinize the testimonies in light of available physical evidence, historical records, and other forms of documentation. This evaluation helps identify any inconsistencies, discrepancies, or factual inaccuracies that may affect the reliability of the testimonies.

## 4. Motives and Bias:

The motivations and potential biases of eyewitnesses should be considered when evaluating their testimonies. Individuals may have personal or cultural motives that could influence the accuracy or objectivity of their accounts. It is essential to assess any potential biases, such as political, nationalistic, or personal interests, which may influence the reliability of the testimonies.

## 5. Time and Memory:

The passage of time can impact the accuracy and reliability of eyewitness testimonies. Memory can be fallible, and details may become distorted or forgotten over time. Eyewitnesses may inadvertently incorporate outside information or popular narratives into their recollections, affecting the credibility of their accounts. Therefore, testimonies provided closer to the time of the events are generally considered more reliable than those provided years or decades later.

## 6. Correlation with Other Evidence:

Eyewitness testimonies should align with other available evidence, such as radio communications, navigational data, historical records, and physical artifacts. Consistency between eyewitness accounts and other forms of evidence increases the credibility and relevance of the testimonies. Corroborating evidence can provide a more comprehensive and coherent understanding of the events.

While eyewitness testimonies can provide valuable insights and clues, they should be evaluated cautiously. The overall strength of the investigation relies on corroborating testimonies, physical evidence, scientific analysis, and a comprehensive approach that considers multiple lines of inquiry. Through diligent analysis and the application of scientific rigor, investigators can determine the credibility and relevance of eyewitness testimonies to the investigation into Amelia Earhart's disappearance.

# VANISHED SKIES: THE MYSTERIOUS DISAPPEARANCE OF AMELIA EARHART

# Chapter 19: International Collaboration and Cooperation

The search for answers regarding Amelia Earhart's disappearance has seen international efforts involving various countries, organizations, and individuals. These international endeavors aim to uncover Earhart's fate and contribute to solving one of aviation's greatest mysteries. Here are some notable international efforts:

As Earhart was an American aviator, the United States has played a significant role in investigating her disappearance. The U.S. Coast Guard and Navy were involved in search and rescue operations at the time of her disappearance. Over the years, U.S. government agencies, including the Federal Aviation Administration (FAA) and the National Transportation Safety Board (NTSB), have continued to support research initiatives, provide resources, and coordinate efforts to uncover the truth.

Australia has been involved in Earhart-related research due to the connection between her final flight and the region. The Australian Maritime Safety Authority (AMSA) and the Australian Transport Safety Bureau (ATSB) have collaborated with international teams in underwater searches and analysis of potential debris fields. The nation's proximity to Earhart's intended flight path has led to Australian researchers and experts contributing to the ongoing investigation.

The United Kingdom has played a role in investigating Earhart's disappearance due to the historical connection with Nikumaroro (then known as Gardner Island). British colonial officials were present on the island after Earhart's disappearance, and subsequent expeditions to Nikumaroro have involved collaboration with British authorities. The UK's involvement has focused on archival research, examination of historical records, and analysis of colonial-era documentation.

Japan has been involved in Earhart-related research due to the potential connection between her disappearance and the Marshall Islands. Researchers have explored the possibility that Earhart and Noonan may have been captured by the Japanese military and taken to the Marshall Islands during the period surrounding their disappearance. Collaborative efforts between Japanese and international researchers have aimed to examine historical records and investigate potential eyewitness testimonies.

International collaboration has been a hallmark of the ongoing search for Earhart. Organizations such as TIGHAR (International Group for Historic Aircraft Recovery) have involved researchers from various countries, fostering collaborative efforts and knowledge sharing. International conferences, workshops, and research forums bring together experts and investigators from around the world to discuss findings, exchange information, and contribute to the collective understanding of Earhart's disappearance.

These international efforts highlight the shared interest and determination to unravel the mystery surrounding Amelia

# VANISHED SKIES: THE MYSTERIOUS DISAPPEARANCE OF AMELIA EARHART

Earhart's disappearance. Collaboration among countries, organizations, and experts from different nations has allowed for a comprehensive and global approach to the investigation. By pooling resources, expertise, and diverse perspectives, these international efforts continue to push the boundaries of knowledge and increase the likelihood of finding answers about Amelia Earhart's fate.

Collaboration has played a crucial role in the ongoing search for answers regarding Amelia Earhart's disappearance. The significance of collaboration lies in its ability to bring together diverse expertise, resources, and perspectives to tackle a complex and enduring mystery.

Collaboration allows for the pooling of resources, both financial and technical, from multiple entities. Governments, research organizations, universities, and individuals can contribute their expertise, specialized equipment, and funding to support the investigation. By leveraging these collective resources, the search can access cutting-edge technologies, conduct comprehensive fieldwork, and perform in-depth analysis that may not be feasible for a single entity.

The mystery surrounding Amelia Earhart's disappearance is multifaceted, requiring insights from various fields, including aviation history, archaeology, forensic science, oceanography, and more. Collaboration brings together experts from these diverse disciplines, fostering an interdisciplinary approach. This collective expertise allows for comprehensive analysis, cross-referencing of evidence, and the application of different methodologies, resulting in a more holistic understanding of the case.

Collaboration facilitates cross-verification and peer review of findings. Researchers and investigators from different backgrounds can scrutinize evidence, evaluate methodologies, and provide critical feedback. This rigorous peer review process helps ensure the credibility and reliability of the investigation's outcomes. The collective effort minimizes biases, errors, and oversights, promoting a more robust and objective analysis.

Collaboration facilitates the sharing of data, information, and historical records among participating entities. Researchers can access previously inaccessible archives, primary sources, and classified documents that may shed light on Earhart's disappearance. The collective effort ensures a broader perspective and reduces duplication of research, saving time and resources.

Collaboration encourages knowledge exchange and the sharing of best practices. Experts from different countries and organizations can share their experiences, methodologies, and insights gained from their respective investigations. This fosters innovation, sparks new ideas, and promotes advancements in technology, analysis techniques, and research approaches. The collective effort allows for continuous learning and the application of the latest advancements in solving the mystery.

The collaboration of international entities brings a global perspective to the investigation. Different countries and cultures may have unique insights, archival records, or eyewitness testimonies that can contribute to the overall understanding of Earhart's disappearance. Collaboration also engages the public, creating a platform for individuals to contribute their knowledge, theories, and personal connections to the case. Public engagement fosters a sense of collective ownership and commitment to finding answers.

In summary, collaboration has been pivotal in advancing the search for answers about Amelia Earhart's disappearance. By pooling resources, expertise, and perspectives, collaboration enables a comprehensive, interdisciplinary approach to the investigation. It facilitates cross-verification, knowledge exchange, and innovation, while also engaging the global community in the pursuit of answers. The significance of collaboration lies in its ability to combine collective efforts, promote rigorous analysis, and increase the chances of solving the enduring mystery surrounding Amelia Earhart.

# Chapter 20: Closure or Continuation: The Enduring Quest

Existing evidence and theories surrounding the disappearance of Amelia Earhart provide insights into the possible fate of the aviator. While no definitive conclusions have been reached, multiple lines of evidence and theories have emerged over the years. Here is a summary of the existing evidence and theories:

## 1. Disappearance Over the Pacific Ocean:

The most widely accepted theory suggests that Earhart's Lockheed Electra ran out of fuel and crashed into the Pacific Ocean near her intended destination, Howland Island. This theory is supported by radio transmissions indicating communication and navigational challenges faced by Earhart and her navigator, Fred Noonan. Despite extensive search efforts at the time, no wreckage or definitive evidence was found.

## 2. Gardner Island (Nikumaroro) Hypothesis:

The hypothesis proposes that Earhart and Noonan made a controlled landing on Gardner Island (now Nikumaroro) and survived as castaways for a period of time. Evidence supporting this theory includes reported radio distress calls, artifacts discovered on the island (such as a woman's shoe and navigational instruments), and the identification of potential aircraft wreckage underwater. However, definitive proof linking these findings to Earhart remains elusive.

### 3. Capture by the Japanese:

Another theory suggests that Earhart and Noonan were captured by the Japanese military while flying near the Marshall Islands. Some eyewitness testimonies and accounts indicate the presence of an American woman resembling Earhart in Japanese custody. However, definitive evidence supporting this theory has not been found.

### 4. Crash Landing on other Islands:

Various accounts propose that Earhart's aircraft may have crash-landed on islands other than Howland Island, such as Mili Atoll or Saipan. These theories rely on eyewitness testimonies, historical records, and reported sightings of aircraft wreckage. However, inconsistencies and challenges in verifying these accounts limit the certainty of their connection to Earhart's disappearance.

### 5. Pacific Islander Oral Traditions:

Oral traditions from Pacific island communities have suggested stories and legends related to Earhart's fate. Some accounts describe the sighting of an aircraft or encounters with individuals fitting Earhart and Noonan's descriptions. While intriguing, the reliability and verifiability of these traditions pose challenges in establishing their connection to Earhart's disappearance.

# VANISHED SKIES: THE MYSTERIOUS DISAPPEARANCE OF AMELIA EARHART

It is important to note that these theories and evidence are subject to ongoing scrutiny, investigation, and reinterpretation as new information arises. The search for definitive evidence and answers regarding Amelia Earhart's disappearance continues, with researchers, organizations, and individuals committed to unraveling the mystery. Advancements in technology, forensic analysis, and collaboration offer hope for future breakthroughs that may provide a clearer understanding of the fate of Amelia Earhart.

The future prospects for finding the truth about Amelia Earhart's disappearance remain hopeful due to several factors:

**1. Advancements in Technology:** Continued advancements in technology, such as improved satellite imagery, underwater exploration techniques, and forensic analysis methods, offer promising avenues for uncovering new evidence. High-resolution imaging, remote sensing, and data analysis techniques may reveal previously undiscovered wreckage or artifacts that could provide crucial clues.

**2. Forensic Techniques and DNA Analysis:** Advancements in forensic techniques, including DNA analysis, have the potential to re-examine existing evidence and possibly identify human remains or artifacts connected to Earhart. Continued improvements in forensic science may lead to breakthroughs in analyzing previously recovered materials or potential discoveries in the future.

**3. Historical Research and Archival Analysis:** Ongoing efforts in historical research and archival analysis may yield new information and insights. Exploration of previously unexplored archives, reevaluation of historical records, and the discovery of overlooked documents could provide critical details about Earhart's flight, communication, or the circumstances surrounding her disappearance.

**4. International Collaboration:** International collaboration among researchers, organizations, and governments continues to bring together diverse expertise and resources. By pooling knowledge, data, and perspectives from around the world, the collective effort enhances the chances of uncovering new evidence, sharing insights, and refining theories. Collaborative endeavors foster innovative approaches and facilitate access to information from different countries and cultures.

**5. Public Engagement and Citizen Science:** Public interest and engagement in the Amelia Earhart mystery remain high. Crowdsourcing initiatives, citizen science projects, and online forums allow enthusiasts, researchers, and individuals to contribute their knowledge, theories, and potential leads. Public participation increases the collective effort in searching for answers and provides opportunities for fresh perspectives and novel discoveries.

**6. Unforeseen Discoveries:** The nature of exploration and discovery often leads to unforeseen breakthroughs. Advances in technology, chance findings, or new research approaches may bring unexpected evidence or insights to light. As technology continues to evolve and new avenues of exploration open up, the possibility of finding key pieces of the puzzle increases.

# VANISHED SKIES: THE MYSTERIOUS DISAPPEARANCE OF AMELIA EARHART

While the mystery surrounding Amelia Earhart's disappearance has endured for decades, the prospects for finding the truth remain promising. The combination of technological advancements, forensic techniques, collaborative research, and public engagement offer hope for future breakthroughs. The dedication of researchers, organizations, and individuals ensures that the search for answers will persist, honoring Earhart's legacy and potentially unraveling one of aviation's most enduring mysteries.

Sign up to my free newsletter to get updates on new releases, FREE teaser chapters to upcoming releases and FREE digital short stories.

Or visit https://tinyurl.com/olanc

I never spam and you can unsubscribe at any time.

# Don't miss out!

Visit the website below and you can sign up to receive emails whenever Oliver Lancaster publishes a new book. There's no charge and no obligation.

https://books2read.com/r/B-A-UNEZ-WHXLC

BOOKS 2 READ

Connecting independent readers to independent writers.

# Also by Oliver Lancaster

Chernobyl: Unveiling the tragedy. A Comprehensive Account of the Nuclear Disaster

The Bhopal Gas Tragedy: Unraveling the Catastrophe of 1984

The Deepwater Horizon Oil Spill of 2010: A Disaster Unveiled

Fukushima Fallout: Unveiling the Truth behind the 2011 Nuclear Disaster

Minamata Disease: Poisoned Waters and the Battle for Justice (1932-1968)

Evil Women: Unmasking History's Most Notorious Women

Bundy The Dark Chronicles: America's Infamous Serial Killer

Dahmer The Dark Chronicles: America's Infamous Milwaukee Cannibal

Zodiac The Dark Chronicles: America's Infamous Cryptic Killer

Bigfoot: The Comprehensive Investigation into the Elusive Legend

Chasing Legends: The Truth behind the Chupacabra

Chasing Legends: The Truth behind the Loch Ness Monster

Aokigahara Forest: The Heartbreaking Secrets of Japan's Suicide Forest

The Amityville House: The Haunting Secrets of America's Most Infamous Residence

The Stanley Hotel: The Mystery of Colorado's Historic
Landmark
The Tower of London: The Haunted Past and Secrets of Royal
Ghosts
The Winchester Mystery House: The Riddle of Sarah
Winchester's Mansion
Vanished Skies: The Mysterious Disappearance of Amelia
Earhart



Watch for more at https://tinyurl.com/olanc.

# **About the Author**

Oliver Lancaster possesses an enchanting charm that effortlessly draws readers into the depths of his literary world. With an insatiable curiosity for the unexplained, he skillfully weaves tales of crime, conspiracy, mystery and the unknown, leaving readers on the edge of their seats.

Nestled away in the seclusion of his garden shed, Oliver finds solace and inspiration in the tranquility of nature. Surrounded by greenery and fragrant blooms, he dives into a realm of imagination, unearthing secrets that lie hidden within his mind.

Accompanying Oliver on his literary ventures is his faithful ginger cat named Italics. With his mesmerizing gaze and mysterious mannerisms, Italics adds an air of intrigue to Oliver's writing process, often curling up on a cushioned chair nearby, watching as words flow effortlessly from his human companion's pen.

When not engrossed in his craft, Oliver indulges in the gentle warmth of his garden with a glass of red wine.

Prepare to be spellbound as you delve into the pages of Oliver Lancaster's novels, for he is a master of the eerie, a weaver of secrets, and an unrivaled guide through the labyrinthine corridors of the human psyche.

Sign up to a free newsletter to get updates on new releases, FREE teaser chapters to upcoming releases and FREE digital short stories.

Read more at https://tinyurl.com/olanc.

www.ingramcontent.com/pod-product-compliance
Lightning Source LLC
Chambersburg PA
CBHW071322150726
47997CB00002B/577